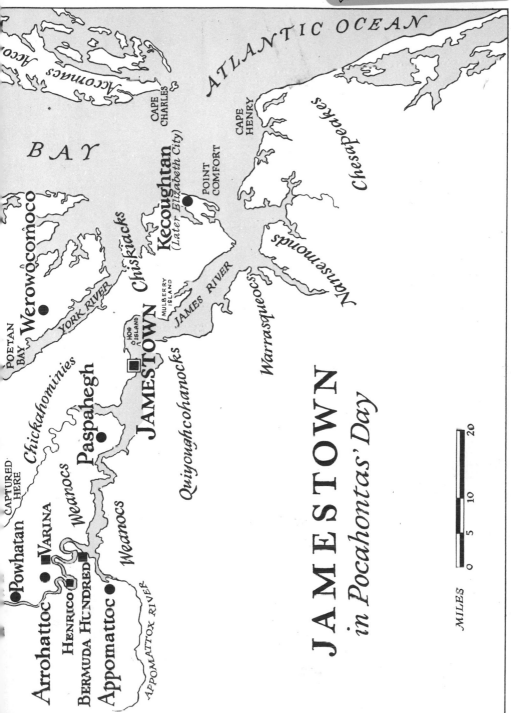

ATLANTIC OCEAN

Accomacs

Accomacs

BAY

CAPE
CHARLES

CAPE
HENRY

Chesapeakes

POINT
COMFORT

Kecoughtan
(Later Elizabeth City)

Werowocomoco

Nansemonds

POETAN
BAY

YORK RIVER

Chiskiacks

Warrasqueocs

Chickahominies

MULBERRY
ISLAND

JAMES RIVER

HOG
ISLAND

JAMESTOWN

Paspahegh

CAPTURED
HERE

Powhatan

VARINA

Weanocs

Quiyoughcohanocks

Arrohattoc

HENRICO

BERMUDA HUNDRED

Appomattoc

Weanocs

APPOMATTOX RIVER

JAMESTOWN
in Pocahontas' Day

MILES

0   5   10   20

THE CIVILIZATION OF THE AMERICAN INDIAN SERIES

Pocahontas

Pocahontas and her son, Thomas Rolfe
(the Sedgeford Hall Portrait).

Pocahontas
by Grace Steele Woodward

University of Oklahoma Press : Norman

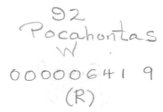
By *Grace Steele Woodward*

The Man Who Conquered Pain: A Biography of William Thomas Greene Morton
   (Boston, 1962)
The Cherokees (Norman, 1963)

Library of Congress Catalog Card Number: 68–15687

Copyright 1969 by the University of Oklahoma Press, Publishing Division of the University. Composed and printed at Norman, Oklahoma, U.S.A., by the University of Oklahoma Press. First edition.

*To Savoie Lottinville,
who made me feel equal to the task*

Acknowledgments

I WISH TO THANK the many thoughtful people who assisted me as I gathered information and data for this book. During the course of my research, both in the United States and in England, seeking out all known historical material relating to Pocahontas' life, I was given great help and guidance by many gracious librarians, scholars, and curators. And though I am indebted to so large a number of institutions and individuals that I cannot name them all, I would like to acknowledge my special gratitude to the following:

The director and staff of the Thomas Gilcrease Institute of History and Art, Tulsa, Oklahoma, and Mrs. Marie E. Keene, the research librarian of the institute; Mrs. Marydell Bradfield, of the Tulsa Central Library; T. Dale Stewart, acting curator of Physical Anthropology, Smithsonian Institution, Washington, D.C.; Robert A. Elder, Jr., museum specialist, Department of Anthropology, U.S. National Museum, Washington, D.C.; the staff of the Library of Congress; the late Eleanor Pitcher, of the Folger Shakespeare Library, Washington, D.C.; the staff of the Virginia State Library, Richmond, Virginia, and the library's archaeologist, Howard A. MacCord; Ben C. McCary, professor of modern languages, the College of William and Mary, Williamsburg, Virginia; The Rev. George J. Cleaveland, registrar of the Diocese of Virginia; Mrs. Wilmer N. Stoneman, present owner of "Varina-on-the-James"; Mary Isabel Fry of the Henry E. Huntington Library and Art Gallery, San Marino, California; His Grace, the Duke of Northumberland, K.G.; A. E. Gunther, collateral descendant of John Rolfe and official historian of the Rolfe family; the staff of Her Majesty's Public Record Office, London; the staff of the British Museum, London, and Edward Croft-Murray of the museum's Department of Prints and Drawings; the staff of the Ashmolean Museum, Oxford University; the staff of the Department of Western Manuscripts of the Bodleian Library, Oxford University; the staff of Magdalene College Library, Cambridge University; Osmond Tudor Francis, friend and guide through England; and Mrs. G. A. Tatchell, wife of the rector of St. George's Church, Gravesend.

I also extend my humble thanks and appreciation to my friends and to the members of my family, who gave me patient understanding and encouragement during the years that were devoted to the research and writing of this biography.

Tulsa, Oklahoma   GRACE STEELE WOODWARD
January 15, 1969

Contents

	Acknowledgments	*page*	*ix*
I.	An Introduction		3
II.	The Powhatans		8
III.	The Invaders		41
IV.	The Beginning of Jamestown		51
V.	The Rescue		63
VI.	Negotiations		74
VII.	Powhatan's Coronation		84
VIII.	The Contest Quickens		92

IX.	The Starving Time	111
X.	A Second Chance	118
XI.	Signs of Success	128
XII.	The Abduction and Conversion	139
XIII.	The Marriage	160
XIV.	A Matter of Money	168
XV.	The Visit to England	174
XVI.	Gravesend	184
XVII.	An Epilogue	187
	Bibliography	196
	Index	215

Illustrations

COLOR PLATES

Pocahontas and her son, Thomas Rolfe (the
Sedgeford Hall Portrait)   *Frontispiece*
Water colors by John White of Indians around
Roanoke (1585):
Village of Secoton   *Page* 19
Indians dancing around a circle of posts   21
Man and woman eating   23

Indians fishing   25
Group of Indians around a fire   27
Village of Pomeioc   29
Pocahontas ("Lady Rebecca") in English court dress
    (the Bootan Hall Portrait)   31
Ruth window, St. George's Church, Gravesend, England   33
Rebecca window, St. George's Church, Gravesend,
    England   35

BLACK AND WHITE PLATES

Water colors by John White of Indians around
    Roanoke (1585):
    Cooking in a pot   101
    Cooking fish   102
    Indian charnal house   103
The "Lyte Jewel," seventeenth-century pendant
    containing a miniature of King James I   104
Captain George Percy   105
Thomas West, Third Lord de la Warr   106
Sir Thomas Dale   107
Eustace Rolfe, grandfather of John Rolfe   108
Frontispiece and title page of John Smith's
    Generall Historie   141
Three illustrations from John Smith's *Generall*
    Historie:
    John Smith as a prisoner of the Powhatans   142
    John Smith capturing the King of the Pamunkeys   143
    Pocahontas rescuing John Smith   144
Powhatan's mantle, a gift to King James I   145
Broadside sent to England from Virginia in 1623   146
Heacham Hall, the Rolfe manor house   146
St. George's Church, Gravesend, England   147

Interior, new St. George's Church, Gravesend,
    England   148
Statue of Pocahontas, St. George's churchyard,
    Gravesend, England   149
Bas-relief of Pocahontas in the Church of St. Mary the
    Virgin, Heacham, Norfolk, England   150
Village road sign commemorating Pocahontas,
    Heacham, Norfolk, England   151
Statue of Captain John Smith, Jamestown, Virginia   152

Pocahontas

CHAPTER I

An Introduction

FOR ABOUT TEN YEARS early in the seventeenth century, Pocahontas, a young Powhatan Indian princess, effected a remarkable and significant relationship first with the small group of English settlers at Jamestown and later with the English rulers and financiers who were sponsoring the colonization of the New World. It was a perceptive and creative relationship that was to help shape the course of American history, for, in her remarkable way, the Powhatan princess helped bring about the ultimate co-operation between her people and the English that was to permit the successful founding of Virginia and lead ultimately to the making of a new nation.

For almost a century before 1607, when the London Company fleet of three small ships landed at Jamestown, the Spaniards had been busy colonizing the New World. They had been active in South America. Cortés had conquered Montezuma and established the rich colony of Mexico. Coronado and De Soto had pushed Spanish claims northward from Florida to California. France had also been deeply interested in the New World. French explorers had moved down the St. Lawrence and into the Great Lakes region, asserting the claims of France to that vast area. England's one small effort at colonization, Roanoke, had disappeared into the caverns of history, a lost and obliterated cause.

For reasons perhaps never to be completely understood, Pocahontas, daughter of Chief Powhatan, negotiated the success of Jamestown and saved it from the fate of the Lost Colony. She saw to it that corn, venison, and other foods were brought to the "gentlemen" colonists, who were ill-prepared to face the hardships of the new land. On a number of occasions she intervened on behalf of the colonists as inevitable conflicts arose between them and the Powhatans. She united her people and the English by her conversion to Christianity and her marriage to John Rolfe. And she represented both English colonist and American Indian when she traveled to the court of James I, there to inspire a greater economic support of colonization in the New World and to educate the British to the reality of a distant place and people.

Pocahontas could not have been much more than ten years old in 1607, when the Jamestown colonists, busily felling trees, clearing ground for gardens, and building their fort, first saw her playing in prenubial nakedness within their settlement, leapfrogging and turning cartwheels with four young cabin boys off

4

the *Susan Constant,* the *Godspeed,* and the *Discovery.*[1] William Strachey, appointed recorder of the colony in 1610, wrote down the stories he heard from earlier colonists about the young girl's visits to Jamestown and her uninhibited game playing with Nathaniel Peacock, James Brumfield, Richard Mutton, and Samuel Collier.[2] After their five-month voyage across the Atlantic (from December 20, 1606, to May 12, 1607), the cabin boys were more than willing to frolic with the energetic Indian princess, who, as Captain John Smith observed, frequented Jamestown in its early days with her "wild traine" as freely as she did her own father's habitation.[3]

Strachey referred to Pocahontas as "a well featured, but wanton yong girl."[4] Smith, on the other hand, apparently saw her not as wanton but as naturally precocious: ". . . a child of tenne years old, which not only for feature, countenance, and proportion exceedeth any of the rest of her people but for wit and spirit [is] the non-pareil of his [Powhatan's] countrie."[5] In light of the events that followed in the ten remaining years of Pocahontas' life, it is understandable that Smith's phrase rather than Strachey's came to be used to describe her. The aristocratic members of the Virginia Company were to appropriate it, and even in later days, when meeting at Sir Thomas Smythe's house on Philpott Lane in London to discuss the management of the

[1] William Strachey, "The First Booke of the Historie of Travaile into Virginia Britania . . .," Cap. 5, 29, MS 1622, Sloane Collection, Department of Manuscripts, Library, British Museum; hereafter cited as "The First Booke." (See also William Strachey, *Historie of Travaile into Virginia Britannia* (ed. by R. L. Major), Cap. V, 65; hereafter cited as *Historie.*)

[2] Strachey, "The First Booke," Cap. 5, 29.

[3] John Smith, *The Generall Historie of Virginia, New-England, and the Summer Isles . . . .*, Book IV, 122; hereafter cited as *Generall Historie.*

[4] Strachey, "The First Booke," Cap. 5, 29.

[5] Edward D. Neill, *Historie of the Virginia Company of London, with Letters to and from the First Colony Never Before Printed,* 83; hereafter cited as *History of the Virginia Company.*

Jamestown colony, the silken-clad members referred to Pocahontas as the "non-pareil of Virginia."

Certainly Pocahontas, from her earliest encounter with the English, was "without equal" among her people as far as her attitude toward the colonists was concerned. The Powhatans in general were fearful and suspicious of the newcomers, and consequently hostile. As early as May 26, only fourteen days after the English arrived, two hundred Paspaheghs, a tribe of Powhatans living near the juncture of the James and Chickahominy rivers, attacked Jamestown, killing Eustis Clovell and wounding eleven other colonists, one of whom later died of his wounds. Throughout the summer of 1607 the deaths of colonists—announced by the booming of artillery from the ships or by cannon or musket fire—prompted the Powhatans to mock and taunt the English. Powhatan warriors yelled and danced in the marsh grass outside the Jamestown fort to celebrate the colony's disasters; the horrendous shrieks and cries of "Yah, ha, ha!" and "Whe, Whe, Whe, Tewittowah"[6] bespoke the Powhatans' contempt for the colonists. In their mocking celebrations the Powhatans would implore their devil-god to plague and destroy the Tassantasses, as they called the English.[7]

Pocahontas did not share her people's hostility, and it is that fact that catapulted her into history. She was a woman who acted contrary to the manner of her people. She made manifest a different attitude, not only toward the English but also toward her own life.[8] Encountering a new culture, she responded with curiosity and concern, and she accepted the potential for change and development within herself. She rose, surely and dramatically, above the ignorance and savagery of her people, whom

---

[6] Strachey, "The First Booke," Cap. 6, 54.

[7] Strachey, *Historie*, Cap. VI, 79.

[8] An attitude that Smith tried to convey by saying, "God made Pocahontas." (John Smith, *New England Trials*, C2.)

6

the Jamestown colonists termed "naked slaves of the devill."[9]
Her story is one of growth—cultural, intellectual, and spiritual.
Her achievement as human being and as maker of history is
extraordinary, and has for too long been obscured in the mists of
legend. It is an achievement that warrants a modern telling and
a new evaluation.

[9] Alexander Whitaker, *Good Newes from Virginia*, 23–24.

CHAPTER II

The Powhatans

To UNDERSTAND POCAHONTAS, one must first understand the Powhatan culture from which she emerged, a culture of dark superstitions and devil worship, a culture of easy cruelty and primitive social accomplishments. Although Pocahontas was exceptional within this culture, nevertheless, in her childhood, she accepted its values and was certainly a witness to, and participant in, the Powhatan way of life. She was, after all, a full-blooded Indian, and, though extremely individualistic within Powhatan society, she was not immune to it. Her later cultural

8

readjustment is all the more significant because she was born when and where she was.

Sometime long before the seventeenth century Pocahontas' people had migrated from the north into the coastal region that is today called Tidewater Virginia, but they kept no historical records carved in stone or inscribed on sticks, nor, unlike many other aboriginal American tribes, did they preserve any legends of their past in oral accounts recited to the succeeding generations. They were a people without a sense of origin or a sense of history.[1]

By Pocahontas' time the Powhatans were established as part of the late Woodland culture that flourished in the southeastern part of what is now the United States. It was a culture of pressure-flaked projectile points, stone-headed hatchets and war clubs, and primitive farm tools constructed of stone or bone. The Woodland "culture" was actually an amalgam of various tribes that belonged to different linguistic families not related by blood, their only common ties being certain tools and implements and other artifactual adaptations to a common environment marked by great stands of pine, cypress, and walnut trees and productive in cleared areas of pumpkin, maize, and beans (*peccatoas*).

The Powhatans lived on the northeastern edge of the Woodland territory. In the coastal and inland areas south and west of the Powhatans were the Cherokees, linguistically linked to the Iroquoian family; the Monacans, linked to the Siouan family; and the Choctaws, Creeks, and Chickasaws, linked to the Muskhogean family. The Powhatans, tied linguistically to the

[1] The prehistoric relics scattered above and below the Powhatan villages do not illuminate the Powhatans' origin. Used, but not made, by Powhatans, these relics—delicately chipped blades in the shape of laurel leaves and finely wrought spears—are thought to have been made by tribes who lived in the Tidewater region more than seven thousand years ago.

9

Algonquians, spoke—slowly and with great deliberation—a dia-
lect derivative of the language spoken by the Algonquians living
on the eastern shore of Chesapeake Bay and in the basins of the
Delaware and Hudson rivers. The Tidewater Powhatans were
distant kinsmen of the Lenape, whose Walam Olum, or "Painted
Tally," told how between 1500 and 1600 bands of Algonquians
settled along the Atlantic Coast from the Strait of Belle Isle, off
the coast of Newfoundland, south to the Savannah River and
also told of the relations among the Mahicans, Munsees, Man-
hattans, and other Indian tribes living along the Hudson River
and near the bays and coastal areas of present-day New York
State.[2]

Not only in language but also in other ways the Powhatans
revealed their Algonquian ties. Like their northern kinsmen, the
Powhatans lived in long, arbor-like houses made by implanting
a double row of saplings in the ground and bending the tops
into an arched roof. The sides of the houses were covered with
mats woven of reeds or with large patches of bark that could be
rolled up or removed in warm weather to permit air to circulate
through the dwellings. The roofs were thatched with marsh
grass or bark. A smoke hole was left in the center of the roof.
Most Powhatan houses had but one large room, though some
tribes built communal houses with one large central room flanked
by several smaller rooms. Houses of these designs were common
among all Algonquian tribes wherever they lived.[3]

There is evidence that sometime before Pocahontas' birth the
Powhatans had established close relations with other displaced
Algonquian tribes living in the Roanoke area in recognition of

[2] Congress, House of Representatives, 82 Cong., 2 sess., *House Report No.
2503,* 509–10; John L. Cotter, *Archeological Excavations at Jamestown,* 6–8; Ben
C. McCary, *Indians in Seventeenth-Century Virginia;* Daniel G. Brinton (ed.),
*The Lenape and Their Legends, with the Complete Text and Symbols of the
Walum Olum.*

[3] McCary, *Indians in Seventeenth-Century Virginia,* 14–16.

and response to their kinship. The Powhatans' primitive swords, usually made of wood or bone, were occasionally made of bog iron similar to that found in deposits near the Outer Banks of North Carolina, not far from Roanoke Island.[4] And the magnificent water-color drawings of the Roanoke Algonquians made by John White in 1585[5] show the similarity of the Powhatans to their Algonquian cousins; the Roanoke tribes pictured in White's seventy-five drawings could easily be mistaken for Powhatans.

A comparison of the water colors with the Jamestown colonists' descriptions of the Powhatans reveals that the appearance and behavior of Roanoke and Powhatan tribes were much the same. For example, the Roanoke warriors depicted by White and described by Thomas Hariot in 1585 were remarkably like the Powhatan warriors described by George Percy two decades later. "The Princes of Virginia," wrote Hariot, . . . "weare the haire of their heads long and bynde opp the ende of the same in a knott under their eares. Yet they cutt the topp of their heads from the nape of the necke in manner of cokscombs."[6] Twenty years later George Percy wrote about the Powhatans: "They shaved the right side of their heads with a shell, the left they weare of an ell [forty-five inches] long tied up with an artifyciall knot, with as many of fowles feathers sticking into it."[7]

According to White's water colors and the Jamestown records, the men and women of both the Roanoke and the Tidewater

[4] Though there were such bog-iron deposits at the falls near Powhatan, a village near the present Richmond (ruled by Parahunt, Pocahontas' half-brother), they were not being extensively mined by the Powhatans at the time Jamestown was founded. It must be concluded that the Powhatans had procured most of the iron for their swords from the Roanoke Island area.

[5] John White, *American Drawings*, Department of Royal Manuscripts, Library, British Museum.

[6] Thomas Hariot, *A Briefe and True Report of the New Found Land of Virginia*, Chap. III.

[7] Samuel Purchas, *Purchas His Pilgrimes*, IV, 1687.

areas had tawny skin shading into light-reddish shades.[8] The men of both areas were about six feet tall, agile, and strong. According to Strachey, the Powhatans had round heads, wide, full-lipped mouths, and broad noses that were "either flatt or full at the end,"[9] characteristics closely resembling those of White's earlier Roanoke models.

Both the White drawings and the Jamestown records indicate that throughout most of the year the Algonquian males wore only breechcloths, consisting of pelts of medium-sized animals with heads and tails intact, fastened to belts and barely covering their "privities," as Strachey expressed it.[10] In winter, however, the men sometimes wore buckskin leggings and moccasins. Elderly men of both the Roanoke and the Tidewater areas wore feather mantles or the skins of wolves, bears, or deer over their shoulders, fastened in such a way as to leave a shoulder and arm bare.

Priests of both regions signified their status by wearing headdresses of dyed deer hair gathered into a topknot crowned with feathers, from which dangled a dozen or more snakeskins stuffed with moss. Knee-length shifts of quilted rabbitskins were their only coverings. In their ears they wore various ornaments: dangling claws of fowls inset with copper, live green garter snakes, or long strands of fresh-water pearls. Their bodies were usually painted black, or black with red or white.

Lesser tribesmen also painted themselves. Even when they were not at war, the tribesmen applied clay mixed with pulverized bloodroot to their faces and bodies. On special occasions walnut oil, blue clay sprinkled with particles of silver ore, white clay, and other ingredients were used for face and body paint.

[8] Strachey wrote, "They are generally of a collour brown or rather tawney." ("The First Booke," Cap. 6, 28.)

[9] *Ibid.*

[10] *Ibid.*

When they prepared for war, warriors of both areas painted identification marks on their shoulders to denote their tribe or village.

On special occasions the women also painted their faces, using a bright-scarlet mixture of berry juice, bloodroot, and other ingredients. Like the men, the women of both regions had long, straight black hair, small black eyes interestingly elongated at the corners, and handsome rather than pretty features. Fond of ornaments, they wore bone necklaces and, depending on their rank, feathers, beads, and other decorations. The chiefs' wives decorated themselves with many strands of pearls interspersed with copper.

Female dress in both the Roanoke and Tidewater areas consisted of a short, apron-like garment of dressed skins, fringed at the lower edges. According to Strachey, upper-class Powhatan women also wore mantles woven of feathers. Strachey described the wife of Pipisco, one of the Powhatan chiefs: ". . . as handsome a salvadge woman as ever I did see," with her mantle of blue feathers "so arteficyally and thick sowed together that it seemed like purple sattan."[11]

Married women of both regions wore their hair "all the same length" over their heads. Unmarried women kept their hair short at the front and sides, "grating it off," as Strachey said,[12] with shells. "Pouncing," or tattooing, the faces, breasts, thighs, and legs in flower, fish, or animal designs was a common practice among the women of both regions.[13]

The striking and picturesque Powhatans practiced a polytheistic religion. According to their creation myth, the Powhatans had been created by a giant hare, who had kept them in a huge bag in a far-distant land where they were constantly

[11] Strachey, *Historie*, Cap. VI, 57–58.
[12] *Ibid.*
[13] *Ibid.*

attacked by a group of aged women. Finally growing weary of the attacks, the hare released the prisoners, who then became earth dwellers. As for death and its aftermath, the Powhatans believed to a certain extent in reincarnation: for werowances, or chiefs, and priests especially, there was to be a continuation of existence; at death their privileged spirits would climb to the top of a tall tree supporting a bridge that led into the sky, where they would live until, after dying a second time, they would be reborn from the womb of an earth woman, to experience a second life on earth.

The most powerful of the Powhatan deities was Okeus, a devil-god, represented by a four-foot idol made of wooden cross-pieces padded with moss, the body painted black, the face flesh-colored or white. Decorated with strands of pearls, the idol occupied the holiest area in each of the Powhatan temples: the chancel at the east and where the priests kept a fire burning to placate the god.

The priests taught that Okeus was responsible for all the evil in the world and that if he was not appeased he would wreak vengeance on the people, visiting sickness upon them, destroying their ripening corn, stirring up wars, making wives false to husbands, and sending storms to ravage their lands. To avoid such catastrophes, the Powhatans made an annual sacrifice of children to the devil-god. The priests would gather the entire Powhatan community in the woods and, after chanting their supplications to Okeus around a great fire, would present two or three of the Powhatan children to the god. Okeus would then mysteriously communicate to the priests the names of those to be sacrificed, and not even the son of a werowance was spared from death on the sacrificial altar if he was unfortunate enough to be selected.

Less powerful than Okeus was Ahone, the Powhatans' beneficent god. Associated with the sun, Ahone did not require

14

placating, but each Powhatan paid homage to the god by bathing in a river or stream each morning at sunrise, following this ritual with another in which he placed dried tobacco in a circle around him, raised his arms skyward to the sun, and then, prostrating himself slowly lowered his hands to the earth. (The colonists, commenting on this ritual, observed that the men howled like wolves and foamed at the mouth.) The Powhatans would also cast bits of deer suet or tobacco into the water before bathing and before eating would spit a fragment of food into the fire as a tribute to Ahone.

— The Powhatan religion was one of ritual—and their ritualistic sense extended to a general delight in celebrations of any kind. In *taquitock*, or autumn, they celebrated the harvest. They observed with dancing and feasting a marriage, the arrival of spring, the appearance of milk in the maize, the flight of wild fowl. Gathering in a circle around a fire, men and women—painted, feathered, and beaded—would dance sensual dances and sing erotic songs, so marking the vital affairs of their lives and the events of nature.

Perhaps the most revealing of their celebrations was the ritualistic torture of captives, a traditional ceremony held by all the Powhatan tribes and on an especially grand scale at the principal Powhatan settlement, Werowocomoco. In preparing for the ceremony, the Powhatan women, who were noted for their cookery, baked maize cakes, broiled fish on hurdles over outdoor fires, roasted joints of venison and wild fowl on spits, and baked fresh oysters in their shells. Wild mulberries, strawberries, and blackberries were included in the menu.

The torture ceremony at which the elaborate meal was served consisted of dismembering bodies of the captives piece by piece while they yet lived. The parts of the bodies were thrown into the fire and eventually reduced to ashes. Sometimes a captive was tied hand and foot and his head laid on a block of stone and beat to a pulp with a stone mallet or a wooden war club. Scalps salvaged from the ceremony were hung on a line stretched between trees—to be admired and appreciated.

Among the Powhatans—savage, ritualistic, and flamboyant— the most powerful and representative figure at the beginning of the seventeenth century was Pocahontas' father, Chief Powhatan himself. He was described by John Smith as "a tall well proportioned man with a sower look, his head somewhat gray, his beard so thin it seemeth none at all, his age near sixtye of a very capable and hardy body to endure any labour."[14] Powhatan was a law unto himself, ruling with dictatorial powers throughout the Tidewater country—as the Jamestown colonists discovered soon after their arrival. After meeting Powhatan, William Strachey remarked that "it is strange to see what great favor and adoration all his people doe obey this Powhatan, for at his feete they present whatsoever he commandeth, and at the least froun of his brow the greatest will tremble, yet may be because he is very terrible and inexorable in punishing such as offend him."[15]

Powhatan had become head of the Powhatans' monarchical government about 1570, succeeding an older brother.[16] Upon his accession Powhatan inherited a small number of tribes and villages: Arrohattoc, twelve miles below the site of present Richmond, on the north bank of the James; Appomattoc, on Swift Creek near present-day Petersburg; Pamunkey, on the neck of land between the Pamunkey River (named the York by the English) and the Mattaponi River; Mattaponi, on the Mattaponi River in what is now King William County; Youghtanund, at the

[14] *Generall Historie*, Book II, 37.

[15] "The First Booke," Cap. 3, 24.

[16] Among the Powhatans the line of succession passed from the oldest brother to the next-oldest. Upon the death of the last brother the succession passed to the oldest sister and her male and female heirs.

Color Plates

Village of Secoton. Water color by John White, 1585. All the White drawings were made of Indians living in the Roanoke region.

Indians dancing around a circle of posts. Water color by John White, 1585.

Man and woman eating. Water color by John White, 1585.

Indians fishing. Water color by John White, 1585.

Group of Indians around a fire. Water color by John White, 1585.

The towne of Pomeiock and true forme of their howses, couered
and enclosed some wth matts, and some wth barcks of trees. All compassed
abowt wth small poles stuck thick together in sted of a wall.

Village of Pomeioc. Water color by John White, 1585.

29

Ætatis suæ 21. Aº. 1616.

National Portrait Gallery, Smithsonian Institution, Washington, D.C.

Pocahontas ("Lady Rebecca") in English court dress (the Bootan Hall Portrait).

Ruth window, St. George's Church, Gravesend, England.
In the lower right corner of the window is a portrait of
Pocahontas in court dress.

Rebecca window, St. George's Church, Gravesend, England, presented by the Colonial Dames of America in 1914. Below the figure of Rebecca is a representation of the baptism of Pocahontas. In the lower right corner is a portrait of Pocahontas in baptismal attire.

head of the Pamunkey River; and Powhatan, a village near the present Richmond and probably Powhatan's birthplace. Apparently about the time of his accession Powhatan changed his name from Wahunsonacock and adopted the name of the village in which he was born.

Soon after 1570, not satisfied to rule the small kingdom he had inherited, Powhatan had conquered twenty-two or more Algonquian tribes in the Tidewater country, annexing their lands. And in the decades before the arrival of the Jamestown colonists, he had welded both inherited and conquered provinces into the powerful Powhatan Confederacy. As the absolute ruler of the confederacy, Powhatan shrewdly placed kinsmen—brothers, sons, and sisters—at the heads of his inherited territories and intimidated the werowances of the conquered tribes until they dared not oppose him.

An example of his intimidation was the night attack he made on the Piankatanks after they resisted his authority. Powhatan slaughtered all the men and carried off the women as captives. On another occasion, when the elderly chief at Kecoughtan (the site of present Hampton) died, Powhatan confiscated his lands, killed the Kecoughtan inhabitants who resisted him, and moved the survivors to Piankatank; then Powhatan transplanted a colony of his own people to Kecoughtan, appointing Pochins, his son, to rule the province.

By 1600 the powerful Powhatan Confederacy, encompassing about 8,500 square miles—about one-fifth of the present state of Virginia—embraced all the lands east of a line from what is now Washington, D.C., through Fredericksburg, Richmond, and Petersburg, Virginia. Southeast along the Blackwater River, the confederacy lands took in that part of coastal North Carolina to the Neuse River. Also included in the confederacy were the present Accomac and Northampton counties, on the eastern shore of Virginia. By 1607 the total population of the confederacy was between 8,500 and 9,000 persons, approximately 3,000 of whom were warriors.[17]

Powhatan ruled the confederacy like a despot. He demanded military support and taxes from all the tribes. The taxes, paid annually, consisted of eight parts out of ten of all the commodities Powhatan's subjects made, grew, or acquired. The skins they trapped, the fish they dried, the crops they raised, the copper they discovered, the pearls they found in oyster and mussel shells, the roanoke (shell beads used as currency) they bartered for—all were taxed.

The pelts, copper, and pearls that Powhatan acquired went into one of his three royal temples at Uttamussack,[18] where they were stored for the day of his death and burial. Piled high within the temple were caskets of pearls, thousands of skins, copper, bows, arrows, elaborately embroidered mantles, and pots of war

[17] The conquered tribes joined the inherited tribes in providing almost complete military protection of the confederacy's boundaries. By the early 1600's, Powhatan had nothing to fear from neighboring enemies, the confederated Manahoacs, a tribe belonging to the Siouan linguistic family, living at the head of the Rappahannock River, and the confederated Monacans, also of the Siouan linguistic family, living at the head of the James River.

Nor did the giant-sized Susquehannas, reputed to be seven feet tall, any longer threaten Powhatan's domain. Belonging to the Iroquoian linguistic family, the Susquehannas were kinsmen of the Iroquois tribes living south and west of the Powhatans, toward the Blue Ridge Mountains. In 1607 the Susquehannas lived north and a little west of the Powhatans. (McCary, *Indians in Seventeenth-Century Virginia*, 81. McCary refers to the Susquehannas [Conestogas] of Maryland, the assumption being that they lived in the Powhatans' area but not in Tidewater Virginia proper. See also Smith, *Generall Historie*, Book III, 60; Strachey, *Historie*, Cap. II, 39; and Charles C. Willoughby, "The Virginia Indians in the Seventeenth Century," *American Anthropologist*, Vol. IX, No. 1 [January–March, 1907], 57. Willoughby points out that the Powhatans were "hemmed in on the south and west by tribes of Iroquoian and Siouan stocks, and were separated on the north from the Canai, or Conoy, and Nanticoke, kindred of the Lenape, from the Susquehannocks, an Iroquoian people, by the Potomac River and Chesapeake Bay.")

[18] Spellings of Indian names are McCary's (*Indians in Seventeenth-Century Virginia*).

paint. Closely guarded on the outside by forty of Powhatan's fiercest warriors, the temple was protected inside by four huge wooden statues, carved in the likeness of a man, a bear, a dragon, and a leopard, standing menacingly in the corners. The taxes paid in grain, fish, dried venison, and other foods went into Powhatan's private storehouse at Werowocomoco, to feed his large family and his guests.

Powhatan not only taxed but also passed laws and issued decrees, one of which was that a man could have as many wives as he could afford. Powhatan himself was reputed to have had more than one hundred wives at one time or another, paying for them with roanoke or with copper, prized by all the Powhatans because of its scarcity. When Strachey visited Powhatan at the chief's large house at Orapaks, sometime between 1611 and 1613, he counted thirty-odd wives, among them Ashetoiske, Amopotoiske, Ponnoiske, Winganucki, and Ottopomtacks.[19]

All in all, Powhatan was a remarkable and powerful leader—fierce, clever, and unscrupulous. By the beginning of the seventeenth century he had made his people not less primitive but certainly more potent and formidable than they had ever been before. He had added ruthless organization and totalitarian methods to their lives. He had aggrandized himself, and he was ready to deal in his own confident and often cruel way with anyone who might challenge his authority.

It was into this world, into the household of Chief Powhatan and into the Powhatan culture, that Pocahontas was born, probably in 1596 or 1597. The colonists believed that Pocahontas' birthplace was Werowocomoco, Powhatan's principal residence until 1609.[20] Which of Powhatan's many wives was Pocahontas' mother is unknown; the mother's name and whereabouts were never ascertained by the colonists, who, in the process of found-

[19] Strachey, *Historie*, Cap. III, 54.
[20] In that year Powhatan became annoyed by the proximity of the colonists

ing Virginia, gathered as many vital statistics about the Powhatans as they could. For all the colonists knew, Powhatan could have had Pocahontas' mother put to death—or, growing tired of her, could have sold her or given her to a werowance in his confederacy to whom he owed some favor. It is more likely that the mother simply went away, since each of Powhatan's wives usually bore him but one child. A century after Pocahontas' death it was rumored that her mother was of "Runic," or Scandinavian, origin—but that is a theory with no real basis and has never been taken seriously by historians or ethnologists.

According to the early colonists, Pocahontas, like all other Powhatans, had two names. Pocahontas, the name given to her by her father, was translated by the English to mean "Bright Stream Between Two Hills" but in the Powhatan tongue perhaps meant "Little Wanton." Her secret name, known only among her own tribesmen, was Matoax, "Little Snow Feather," a name conjuring up the image of a slim, amber-skinned girl enveloped from neck to knee in a mantle woven of snow-white feathers plucked from the breast of a wild swan. Such a mantle, worn by Pocahontas in winter with moccasins and leggings of finely dressed white skins, would have given her people ample reason for calling her Matoax.

Pocahontas had her public and her secret names. She had her place in the Powhatan tribe. She was a favorite daughter in her father's home. As a princess, she was as privileged within the Powhatan world as anyone besides her father could be. And certainly she was heiress—indeed a royal heiress—to her people's attitudes, beliefs, and prejudices. It would be expected, therefore, that she would share in the general Powhatan distrust of white-skinned strangers and in her father's particular hatred of anyone who came to his land from across the sea.

---

and moved to Rasawrack, near Orapaks, his former hunting lodge, located between the Chickahominy and Pamunkey rivers, in what is now New Kent County.

CHAPTER III

The Invaders

By the time the English colonists arrived on the Virginia shore in 1607, the Powhatans were smoldering with a resentment that had its roots in a number of earlier visits by white men to their territories. For almost a century Europeans had been making sporadic visits to Powhatan country, and though some of the encounters had been amicable, others had resulted in misunderstanding at the best and sharp enmity at the worst.

Aged Powhatans living near the mouths of the four great rivers—the Potomac, the Rappahannock, the Pamunkey, and

Powhatan's Flu[1]—that striped the Powhatans' domain and emptied into Chesapeake Bay could remember seeing throughout their lifetimes various ships, flying French, Spanish, and possibly English flags, anchored offshore. Throughout the sixteenth century explorers from Europe had been attracted to the excellent natural harbors of the Powhatans. In 1524, Giovanni da Verrazano, the dark-bearded Florentine explorer who had been commissioned by Francis I of France to explore the New World, had led his fleet into Chesapeake Bay. His stay was short and disinterested, however, for he had already planted the French flag on the windswept sand dunes of the North Carolina coast near Cape Hatteras and Cape Fear.

A more colorful visit was that made in 1525 by Estéban Gómez, who arrived on Powhatan soil to claim the land for Spain.[2] The military drums, the clang of armor, the flash of silver helmets, the gleaming tips of spears, glaives, and maces, the harquebusiers in their slashed and ribbed uniforms—all these sights and sounds on the wilderness shore made an impressive spectacle for the Powhatans watching from hiding places behind sand dunes and in the marsh grasses. In a ceremony epitomizing the glory and power of Spain, the "conquerors" stood at attention as Gómez exclaimed proudly, "I possess all the new western world, in the name of our Lord Charles V." Gómez did not stay to exploit or administer the Powhatan territory, however, and the Powhatans were not yet faced with the problem of dealing with Europeans.

The Spanish were to return. Around 1560 Captain-General Pedro Menéndez de Avilés and his Spanish adventurers landed

[1] The James River, called Powhatan's River or Powhatan's Flu on the maps drawn by Captain John Smith.

[2] Reuben Gold Thwaites (ed.), *The Jesuit Relations and Allied Documents, 1612–1614*, II, 251–52; J. Bartlett Brebner, *The Explorers of North America, 1492–1806*, 115; James Mooney, "The Powhatan Confederacy, Past and Present," *American Anthropologist*, Vol. 9, No. 1 (January–March, 1907), 123–29.

on the Powhatan coast, captured the son of a werowance, and made him a slave. Menéndez became interested in the youth and took him to Cuba, to Mexico, and finally back to Spain, where the boy was educated in the finest schools and converted to the Roman Catholic faith. Upon his conversion he was given the name Don Luis de Velasco, in honor of the Spanish viceroy in Mexico. Pensioned by Philip II, Don Luis for a time lived the life of a Spanish grandee. Then in 1565 he returned to the New World to serve in Florida as interpreter for Menéndez during the construction of the fort at St. Augustine. Because of his outward conformity to Spanish customs, Don Luis was next chosen by Menéndez to help establish the Roman Catholic faith in Powhatan country—a country Don Luis had not seen since his abduction.

Don Luis was sent with an expedition headed by Father Juan Segura, a Jesuit missionary, who, refusing a military escort entered Indian country with nine other missionaries. The expedition entered Chesapeake Bay in the fall of 1570 and landed to celebrate Mass at the site of present-day Newport News, Virginia. Then, guided by Don Luis, Father Segura and the other missionaries, accompanied by a Spanish youth named Alonzo de Olmos, sailed up the James to the mouth of College Creek. Crossing the site of present-day Williamsburg, they eventually reached a point at the mouth of Queens Creek adjacent to the Pamunkey River. Here, with the help of Don Luis, Father Segura built a house to be used both as a residence and as a mission—the first such building on Powhatan land.

But the Spanish missionaries had not reckoned on Don Luis' reaction to his return to the land of his people. Instead of helping convert the Powhatans, Don Luis reverted to savagery. Using the Jesuits' own axes, he and several Powhatan accomplices murdered all the members of the expedition except Olmos, who escaped and found shelter with friendly Indians in the present

43

Hampton, Virginia, area. In 1572, Olmos was rescued by a Spanish relief ship whose captain avenged the murder of the missionaries by hanging a number of innocent Indians from the ship's yardarms before setting sail for Cuba.[3]

This episode marked the end, for the time being, of Spain's interest in colonizing the Powhatan region. It also marked the growing shadow of conflict between the indigenous Indian and the invading European, a conflict whose outcome was not yet predictable.

By the 1580's the Powhatan priests were prophesying that enemies would someday invade from the east through Chesapeake Bay and destroy the Powhatan people. Chief Powhatan, busy at the task of building and ruling his confederacy, was determined to prevent the fulfillment of the prophecy. He launched a campaign that eliminated nearly all the Chesapeake Indians living east of him, and he may well have been instrumental in the extermination of the Roanoke colony as well. That colony, founded on Roanoke Island in 1584, was re-established in 1587 (after all the original colonists had returned to England), but had disappeared by 1591, when its former governor, John White, returned from a stay in England. Certainly the Powhatans had had reason to hate the Roanoke colonists. Sir Richard Grenville, whose crested silver goblet had been stolen by an Indian, had retaliated by burning the offender's village to the ground. Ralph Lane, during his terms as governor of Roanoke Island, had burned a great many more native villages in reprisal for minor thefts.[4] Later colonists in Virginia were convinced that Powhatan —to avenge these deeds or to prevent further conflict—had been involved in what was probably a massacre of the entire Roanoke community.[5]

[3] Clifford M. Lewis, S.J., and Albert J. Loomis, S.J., *The Spanish Jesuit Mission in Virginia, 1570–1572*, 15–55.
[4] *History of the Thirteen Colonies*, 44.

By the beginning of the seventeenth century, during the years of Pocahontas' infancy and early childhood, the Powhatans' apprehensions about the Europeans had matured into an easily inflamed hostility. In 1604 a white man—his name unknown to history—was to provide one more aggravating event that led eventually to the drama in which Pocahontas played a leading role.

Paddling up the Rappahannock and Pamunkey rivers, the white man and his companions accepted the hospitality of a number of Powhatan werowances along their route, particularly the werowances of the Pamunkey, Rappahannock, and Chickahominy tribes. The hospitality offered to the party was not unusual, according to later accounts, even though the Powhatans were as a group fearful and anxious about strangers. Certain Powhatans were willing to observe and make contact with visi-

[5] Strachey, *Historie*, Cap. VIII, 101–102. The Jamestown colonists, having been so instructed by James I, made a serious effort to solve the mystery of Raleigh's second colony, though their only clue was the word "Croatoan" carved on a tree on Roanoke Island. When rumors reached the Jamestown colonists that Powhatan himself had been involved and that four men, two boys, and one girl had survived Powhatan's massacre of the colony, the colonists became increasingly watchful for English survivors. One rumor persisted that the survivors had been whisked off to an out-of-the-way village, where they were engaged in teaching Powhatan's people how to make brick and glass, later they heard the disheartening rumor that Powhatan, fearing the Roanoke survivors would be rescued by the Jamestown colonists, had ordered them killed.

Around May 20, 1607, while exploring the James River, Christopher Newport, captain of the *Susan Constant*, and his party made an exciting discovery, as recorded by George Percy, a member of the party: "At Port Cotáge in our voyage up the River we saw a Savage Boy about the age of tenne yeares which had a head of haire of perfect yellow and reasonable white skinne which is a miracle amongst all savages." (Purchas, *Purchas His Pilgrimes*, IV, 1689.) The Newport party believed that the boy was a Roanoke descendant but failed to make contact with him.

Discouraged by their failure to learn anything definite, and busy with their own settlement, the Jamestown colonists finally gave up their search for the Roanoke survivors.

tors to their country. On this occasion the visitors were beckoned
to shore by the hospitable (and curious) chief of the Rappahannocks and seated on mats of woven reeds. Then the chief delivered an oration with great gusto and much gesticulation.
Tubular clay pipes filled with tobacco grown and dried by the
Powhatans were lighted and passed to the visitors. Then came
feasting, dances, and games.⁶

The visitors, however, were little interested in entertainments
or feasting. Their primary purpose was to abduct likely-looking
young Powhatan boys to be sold as slaves to West Indies plantation owners. On this occasion they abducted a young Powhatan,
apparently the son of the werowance who had entertained them.
As the story was later told, the wrathful father and his warriors
shot at the escaping whites, but their arrows broke against the
enemies' metal armor. The whites then turned their guns on
the Indians, killing the werowance and many of his warriors.⁷
After this incident, and others like it, the Powhatans seized every
opportunity to procure the white men's weapons, especially their
guns. In later encounters with white men, the Powhatan chiefs
signaled them to lay down their arms before coming ashore,
promising that their warriors would do the same. But the command was seldom heeded.

It is not surprising that the Powhatans were resentful and
suspicious when in 1607 a new group of Europeans arrived on
their shores—the Englishmen who were to found Jamestown.
The Powhatans recalled the Spanish and English slave hunters
who had preyed upon them. They recalled their difficulties with
the Roanoke colonists. They recalled the syphilis that the white
men had brought to them, a disease against which the Powhatans' remedies of herbs and roots and incantations and sacrifices had been unavailing and which had brought suffering and

⁶ Smith, *Generall Historie*, Book II, 30–34; Strachey, *Historie*, Cap. VI, 78.
⁷ Philip Barbour, *The Three Worlds of Captain John Smith*, 163.

death to many Indians.[8] With the arrival of a new group of Europeans, the tribal priests reiterated their warnings to Chief Powhatan. If he did not resist the "enemies from the east," his people would be compelled to sacrifice thousands of their male children to Okeus. All the people of the Powhatan Confederacy would be in great danger if the new invaders were not resisted and driven out.

The English colonists were not aware of the difficult situation in which they were placing themselves. Even with the Roanoke disaster in mind, the Jamestown colonists were filled with hope as they ventured into what they considered to be an inevitable and necessary historical experience. With the accession of James I to the throne of England in 1603, New World colonization had become a matter of intense concern to the English. They had long worried about Spain's power in the New World, but because of internal strife and foreign wars their exploration and colonization efforts had largely been restricted to private ventures. By the early 1600's many powerful arguments were put forth to justify government-supported colonization: England, with a population of four million, was overcrowded. The defeat of the Spanish Armada had forced Spain to retreat from her century-long leading role in New World colonization. The time was ripe to assert England's rights to part of the wealth across the ocean. Moreover, the conversion of the Indians to the Anglican faith was imperative if the New World was not to fall under the hegemony of the Roman Catholic Church.

Consequently, on April 10, 1605,[9] the Great Seal of England was affixed to the first Virginia charter, and the stage was prepared for an encounter not only between individual Europeans

[8] Letter from George Thorpe to John Ferrar, 1621, MS 1019, John Ferrar Papers, Department of Manuscripts, Library, Magdalene College, Cambridge University; Strachey, *Historie*, Cap. IV, 110; Cotter, *Archeological Excavations at Jamestown*, 23–24.

[9] William W. Abbot, *A Virginia Chronology, 1585–1783*, 2.

and Indians but also between the English government and the Powhatan Confederacy.

The charter actually provided for two colonizing groups, one to settle North Virginia (New England) and the other to settle South Virginia (the present Tidewater Virginia region). The colonization of South Virginia was backed primarily by Londoners: Sir George Somers, an expert navigator; Richard Hakluyt, the renowned geographer; Edward Maria Wingfield, an experienced military leader; and Sir Thomas Smythe, one of the most astute businessmen of the day. Smythe was made treasurer of the group, which was henceforth known as the Virginia Company of London.

Soon after the charter was signed, King James issued the Articles and Instructions for the Virginia colony.[10] Described by his enemies as "the wisest fool in Christendom," James had one real gift—the ability to concentrate on an issue long enough to produce a treatise of intellectual and practical worth. With the help of Sir John Popham, lord chief justice of England, and other English intellectuals, James outlined clearly and concisely the procedure for the colonists to follow in establishing the settlements in North and South Virginia.

The instructions for South Virginia were sealed in three boxes, one of which was placed aboard each of the three outward-bound ships. When the ships dropped anchor in Chesapeake Bay, near present Cape Henry, in April, 1607, the instructions were opened and read. They dealt with, among other things, the choice of a site for settlement; the treatment of the Indians, or "naturals"; the exploration of the rivers and lands of the region; the fortification of the settlement; the recovery of the lost Roanoke colony; the search for natural resources that would bring wealth to England; and the discovery, if possible, of a route to the "Indian Sea." The instructions also contained the names of

[10] MS 21993, fol. 187, British Museum Archives; Abbot, *Chronology*, 2.

the members of the Jamestown council, as well as the name of its first president, Edward Maria Wingfield. To prevent the seeds of Catholicism from being planted in the new colony, each member of the council was required to take an oath of allegiance to King James, thereby renouncing allegiance to the pope.[11]

Thus well instructed, officially chartered, properly sworn, and representing the English nation and culture more explicitly than any group had ever done before, the Jamestown colonists confronted the Powhatan Indians, who were prepared, for their own reasons and in their own fashion, to complicate the English goal of an easy, immediate, reasonable, and rewarding establishment of the English way of life in the New World.

For the first days after the Jamestown colonists arrived, there were no overt acts of hostility. The Quiyoughcohanocks (Tapahanocks), who lived on the south bank of the James River, seemed friendly, as did the Paspaheghs, who lived west of the Chickahominy River near the point where it joined the James. Moreover, Pochins, Pocahontas' half-brother and the werowance at Kecoughtan, entertained the colonists lavishly when they visited his village while seeking a site for the settlement.

Then on May 18, four days after the colonists' arrival, an incident occurred that tragically altered relations between the Powhatans and the English—an incident that might have been

---

[11] Manuscript Records of the Virginia Company, Vol. III, Part i, 20, 20a, Library of Congress List of Records No. 5. The oath of Allegiance reads: "I, M_____ doe utterlie testifie & declare in my conscience y^t y^e kings highnes y^e onlie supreame Governor of Great Brietaine and of all the Collouy . . . in all spirituall [and] ecclesiasticall things (or causes) as temporall. . . ." The oath of Supremacye reads: "I _____ M_____ doe trulie and sincerely acknowledge, professe testifie and declare in my Conscience before God & the world, That our Soveraigne Lord King . . . ys lawful and rightfull King of great Britaine and of the Colony of Virginia, and of all other his Maiesties Dominions and Countries. And that y^e pope neither of himselfe, nor by any Authoretie of the Church or See of Rome, or by any other meanes . . . hath any power or authorictie to depose the King or to dispose of any of his Maiesties Kingdomes or Dominions. . . ."

avoided if the colonists had been wiser and more tolerant of Powhatan ways and if the Powhatans had not been prepared to see in these particular Englishmen the enemies they desperately feared.

On that day the werowance of Paspahegh, accompanied by one hundred warriors, paid an ostensibly friendly visit to the colonists, bringing with him "a fat Deare"[12] for a feast. As the incident was recorded by George Percy, at first all went well at the meeting between the werowance and the colonists. The chief asked the white men to lay down their guns but did not seem particularly upset when they refused to do so. He even made signs—or so it seemed to the colonists—that he would give them all the land they wanted for their settlement. At that moment one of the settlers caught sight of a warrior making off with his English hatchet. According to Percy, the colonist "tooke it from him by force, and also strooke him over the arme. Presently another Salvage seeing that, came fiercely at our man with a wooden sword thinking to beat out his braines. The werowance of Paspahegh saw us take to our arms, and went suddenly away with all his company in great anger."[13]

It was an ominous beginning for the colonists, and to the Powhatans it was the long-dreaded invasion from the east. On May 26 the Paspaheghs attacked Jamestown. Thus the conflict was engaged, producing hostility that sometimes flared into warfare. The fate of Jamestown and Virginia, and all that they were finally to represent, depended upon a resolution that in 1607 was nowhere in sight.

[12] Purchas, *Purchas His Pilgrimes*, IV, 1688.
[13] *Ibid.*

CHAPTER IV

The Beginning of Jamestown

DURING THE FIRST DIFFICULT DAYS, weeks, and months of the English settlers' efforts to establish their colony, Pocahontas began what was to be her education in a new way of life and also began, to the future benefit of the English, what was to be her comprehension of that way of life and its relationship to the life of her people. Even in the midst of potential war and various acts of divisiveness between her people and the colonists, she ventured onto Jamestown Peninsula—a low-lying, unpleasant place abandoned by the Powhatans untold years earlier because of its vulnerability to hurricanes—to observe with her perceptive eyes the behavior and activity of the men from across the sea, struggling to build an orderly community.

No doubt Pocahontas watched in some amazement as the colonists erected a church, a fort, and habitations unlike anything she had seen before. Actually the buildings that impressed Pocahontas were by English standards quite primitive. According to Captain Smith, "For a Church we did hang an awning (which is an old sail) to three or foure trees to shadow us from the sunne. Our walls were rales of wood, our seats unhewed trees, till we cut plankes, our Pulpit a bar of wood nailed to two neighboring trees."[1] The fort itself was somewhat more substantial. It was built by laborers such as John Laydon, William Cassen, and "Old Edward," who felled tall trees for lumber and, with the help of the carpenters—William Laxton (or Laxon), Edward Pising, Thomas Emry, and Robert Small—completed the fort, which enclosed a storehouse, a market place, and several streets. When the fort was finished on June 15, George Percy noted that it was "triangle wise, having three Bulwarkes at every corner like a Halfe Moone, and foure or five pieces of Artillerie mounted in them."[2] No doubt Pocahontas was intrigued by the white men's buildings and also by their tools—the metal axes, hatchets, knives, and saws—and the weapons they kept close at hand—guns, poleaxes, pikes, demiculverins, and cannon. Certainly for Pocahontas the Jamestown settlement was a center of strange and exciting activity and, since she was but a child, a center of friendly attention from a remarkable and fascinating people.

Pocahontas may or may not have seen white men before 1607,

[1] John Smith, *Advertisements for the Unexperienced Planters of New England, or Anywhere: Or, the Path-Way to Experience to Erect a Plantation,* 32; hereafter cited as *Advertisements.*

[2] Purchas, *Purchas His Pilgrimes,* IV, 1689.

but even if she had, the English colonists would still have been curiosities. The English were shorter than the Powhatan men, and many of them had beards and mustaches. They dressed in peculiar ways, the Powhatans derisively called them "coat-wearing people." The colony's laborers wore jerkins of coarse home-spun linen or canvas with matching breeches or hose, the dress prescribed by Parliament for their class in the time of Elizabeth I. The everyday dress of the Jamestown gentlemen, though not elaborate, was noticeably finer than the clothes the laborers wore on the Sabbath. The gentlemen's Sunday clothes were the finest in Jamestown: satin or taffeta lavishly decorated with slashes, pinking, and embroidery. The gentlemen's Sunday hats were plumed, while the laborers wore either small, flat berets like those worn by London craftsmen and known as "city flat caps" or brimmed hats with the severest of crowns, which had come into style in the latter part of the sixteenth century. On Sundays the gentlemen wore shoes of cordovan leather, while the laborers exchanged their sturdy boots for clumsy, heavy-soled shoes. When summer arrived, the gentlemen were compelled to shed their heavy, lined doublets, and the laborers, their jerkins.[3]

When Pocahontas first began visiting the colony, it contained more than one hundred Englishmen, and she soon became known to them all: the forty-eight English gentlemen, the Anglican chaplain, and the twelve laborers, the four carpenters, the bricklayer, the mason, the tailor, the blacksmith, the barber, and "divers others"[4] whose names, for some reason, were not listed on the ships' passenger lists.

Among the colonists were a number of especially interesting

[3] "Bill for Necessaries Bought by Mr. George Percy for His Voyage to the West Indies," MS Aln 114/5, Manuscripts, Dukes of Northumberland, Library of Congress (microfilm); Virginia A. LaMar, *English Dress in the Age of Shakespeare.*
[4] Smith, *Generall Historie,* Book III, 43–44.

and enterprising men. Among them was George Percy, a lean-faced, clean-shaven (except for a small mustache), member of the English aristocracy.[5] Percy had left England to escape persecution by King James. He was the younger brother of the ninth Earl of Northumberland—called the "Wizard Earl" because of his interest in science—who had been imprisoned for several years in the Tower of London for alleged participation in the Gunpowder Plot to blow up the House of Lords—and also the king. George Percy, knowing that he had no future in England while James ruled, preferred seeking his fortune elsewhere to joining his brother in the Tower. Another prominent colonist was John Ratcliffe, captain of the *Discovery* and a member of the Jamestown council, a man whom John Smith dubbed a "counterfeit Impostor"[6] after it was discovered that Ratcliffe's real name was Sicklemore. Though he was surrounded by an aura of mystery, apparently Ratcliffe had not adopted the alias for any ulterior purpose; Ratcliffe was the name of his stepfather, and Sicklemore, that of his true father, who was dead.

The newly elected president of the council, forty-seven-year-old Edward Maria Wingfield,[7] a member of an aristocratic Catholic family, was perhaps the most prestigious of the colonists. A military man who had served in Ireland and the Low Countries, Wingfield had been considered by the King's Council sufficiently experienced to carry out its instructions. However, Wingfield's Catholicism was held against him by the colonists, even though he had joined the other council members in taking the oath of allegiance.

There were other reasons for Wingfield's unpopularity. He

[5] MSS Aln 114/5, Aln 3/2, Aln 4/1, Aln 4/2, Manuscripts, Dukes of Northumberland, Library of Congress (microfilm); *Syon House*, 16–18.

[6] Smith, *Generall Historie*, Book III, 72.

[7] Henry Chandlee Forman, "Jamestown and St. Mary's Buried Cities of Romance," 35n.

was opinionated and brusque and impractical. At first he had been reluctant to fortify Jamestown for fear that to do so would wound the sensibilities of the Indians. When the Paspaheghs attacked the colony, Wingfield had second thoughts, reinforced by a Paspahegh arrow that hissed through his well-tended beard.

By far the most intriguing personality in the Jamestown colony was Captain John Smith, a dashing young bachelor of twenty-six, with twirled mustache and neatly trimmed beard. Smith had been a soldier of fortune in foreign lands before coming to Jamestown. He later boasted that "the warres in Europe, Asia, and Africa taught me how to subdue the Salvages in Virginia."[8] En route to Jamestown on the *Susan Constant* he had been arrested and put in irons by Captain Newport, who had accused him of inciting mutiny among some of the ship's passengers. Smith was released soon after the colonists landed at Jamestown, but he was not permitted to take the oath of allegiance to King James or to sit with the council, of which Newport was an honorary member, until June 10, when he was cleared of the charges against him.[9]

John Smith was not only the most intriguing of the colonists but also, as far as the young Pocahontas was concerned, the most approachable. From the time he began participating in colonial affairs, Smith was aware of the need for communication between the English and the Indians. He took the initiative in learning the Powhatan language so that he and the other colonists could talk with their hostile neighbors. For her part, while most of the Powhatans were uninterested in communicating with the English, Pocahontas also tried to penetrate the language barrier. Using the signs of her language, she would place her left hand over her heart and raise her right arm, a sign taken by the col-

[8] Smith, *Advertisements*, 1.
[9] John Smith, *Travels and Works of Captain John Smith* (ed. by Edward Arber and A. G. Bradley), II, 388.

onists to mean, "I am your friend," "I speak the truth," or "I will keep my promise."[10]

Smith's interest in learning the Powhatan language, and Pocahontas' youthful willingness to communicate, enabled him to learn from her a number of Powhatan words, phrases, and sentences, such as *tomahacks*, meaning "axes"; *monacookes*, meaning "swords"; *pawpecones*, meaning "pipes"; and *pawcussacks*, meaning "guns." Smith also learned that Pocahontas' people could count to one thousand, by ones to ten, and then by tens to one thousand.[11] His study of the Powhatan language lasted from 1607 to 1609 and resulted in a Powhatan vocabulary that he included in his *Generall Historie*. Smith composed sentences in English and then translated them into Powhatan. One of the most interesting of his practice sentences was, "Kekaten Pokahontas Patiaquagh niugh tanks Manotyens neer mowchick rawrenock Audough," which meant, according to Smith, "Bid Pokahuntas bring hither two little baskets, and I will give her white beads to make her a chaine."[12]

It was from Smith that Pocahontas learned her first English words—and received her first English "jewels." Both gifts, intellectual and material, marked the beginning of Pocahontas' friendship with Smith, the friendship that was later to prove invaluable to the dashing young captain.

Smith's concern with language was, of course, utilitarian, part of his plan for accommodation to the New World. The colonists' gifts to the Indians (the treasurer of the Virginia Company had seen to it that they had plenty of glass beads, bells, brass pans, metal hatchets, axes, and saws for trading) were also part of the design for success in the colonization effort. But words and beads alone were not to be adequate in the face of obstacles as formidable as the American wilderness and the recalcitrant natives.

[10] Purchas, *Purchas His Pilgrimes*, IV, 1690.
[11] Smith, *Generall Historie*, Book II, 40.   [12] *Ibid.*

In a very short time the colonists realized that their survival was threatened and that some determined counter measures were in order. The primary problem was the Indians, of course, and one measure that seemed to be indicated was the conversion of the Powhatans to Christianity. The Reverend Robert Hunt, the Anglican chaplain, believed that the way to tame the savages was to bring them into the Anglican faith, with its services centered around the Bible, the Book of Common Prayer, and the Constitution and Canons of the Province of Canterbury, from which Mr. Hunt read to his congregation on the Sabbath and other holy days. A special prayer had been composed for the colonists, and by the king's command it was said each morning and evening. The prayer clearly revealed the attitude of the English toward their pagan neighbors:

> Almighty God, . . . seeing that thou hast honoured us to choose us out to bear thy name unto Gentiles, we therefore beseech thee to bless us and this plantation which we and our nation have begun in thy fear and for thy glory . . . and seeing Lord, the highest end of our plantation here is to set up the standard and display the banner of Jesus Christ, even here where Satan's throne is, Lord let our labour be blessed in labouring for the conversion of the heathen. . . . Lord sanctify our spirits and give us holy hearts, that so we may be thy instruments in this most glorious work.[13]

Other colonists, among them Captain Smith, were not convinced that religious conversion would eliminate the problem with the Powhatans. They believed that it was necessary to subdue the Indians, though that would not be easily achieved either, for the colonists were not especially effective as soldiers in the Powhatans' native territory. The colonists had brought with them suits of light armor, which were impractical in the hot,

[13] Rev. G. Maclaren Brydon, *Highlights Along the Road of the Anglican Church*, 8.

humid weather that enveloped Jamestown Peninsula. The metal skirts, breastplates, and helmets were not only uncomfortably hot but also difficult to get into quickly during an Indian attack. The colonists' heavy matchlock muskets, which had to be propped on rests to be fired, were suitable for formal European warfare but as impractical as armor for informal combat with Indians, who, hiding in the tall marsh grass, sent arrows flying into the midst of the colonists as they worked in their gardens, gathered reeds, or felled trees. Long before a colonist could pour black powder into the muzzle of his musket, follow it with a two-ounce lead ball, and ram the charge home with a long iron ram-rod, he was dead from Indian arrows. So many colonists died in the early months of the settlement that the artillery in the fort and on the ships had to be pressed into service to repel the Indians. Poleaxes, pikes, and swords were also useless in the kind of warfare waged in the Virginia wilderness. How could one charge an enemy who was lying on his belly in the swamp, hidden from view by grass?

At the same time the colonists were confronted with the seemingly unresolvable Indian problem, they were also confronted with the problem of depleted supplies and provisions. It was decided that Captain Newport would return to England with the *Susan Constant* and the *Godspeed* and bring back sorely needed supplies. On Sunday, June 21, 1607, the colonists celebrated Communion, and the gentlemen finished off the day at a farewell dinner given by Captain Newport in his quarters aboard the *Susan Constant*. The next day Newport sailed.[14]

14 Abbot, *A Virginia Chronology, 1585–1783*, 3. Captain Newport, who had lost an arm in the service of his country, was a capable man, and his qualifications for his job were a matter of record, as was his discipline of his ship. His main responsibility was to ferry colonists and supplies across the Atlantic, and between voyages he was to explore the surrounding country, looking for the natural wealth the New World offered. On this return voyage Newport's ships carried pine planks to be used for wainscoting in English manor houses (planks

The day after the ships departed, George Percy noted in his diary: "Captain Newport being gone for England, leaving us (one hundred and foure persons) verie bare and scantie of victualls, furthermore in warres [among ourselves] and in danger of the Salvages. We hoped after a supply which Captaine Newport promised within twentie weeks."[15] Thomas Studley, who was in charge of the storehouse at Jamestown, noted that the food remaining for the colonists was scanty and unappetizing. He reported that "there remained neither taverne, beerhouse, nor place of reliefe but the common Kettle . . . and that was halfe a pint of wheat, and as much barley boyled with water, for a man a day."[16] Percy tried to be optimistic, describing in his diary the "fruitfulness" of the new country and praising the James River: "If this river which wee have found had beene discovered in the time of warre with Spaine, it would have beene a commoditie to our Realme, and a great annoyance to our enemies."[17] But Percy's optimism could not hide the fact that provisions were fast disappearing.

In addition to the problems of the Powhatans and the lack of food, the colonists were beset with yet another difficulty, strife among themselves. After Newport's departure, Wingfield grew more unpopular than ever. He bunged up the two gallons of sack and aqua vitae left by Newport for the Communion table. He showed little concern for the colonists' hunger, suggesting that if they wanted more food they could fish or hunt for it. Sturgeon, pike, and other varieties of fish were available, and there was plenty of wild game and fowl. But because of the increasing hos-

cut by colonists who were still sleeping on the ground at Jamestown), as well as specimens of earth obtained around Jamestown to be analyzed for gold, and batches of sassafras to be tested for its curative powers in the treatment of syphilis.

15 Purchas, *Purchas His Pilgrimes*, IV, 1689.

16 Smith, *Generall Historie*, Book III, 44.

17 Purchas, *Purchas His Pilgrimes*, IV, 1689.

tility of the Indians few colonists dared venture beyond the fort. In various ways Wingfield proved an unsatisfactory leader, and finally he was removed from his office as president of the council by vote of John Smith, John Ratcliffe, and John Martin. Ratcliffe was elected president in his place.[18]

Also contributing to the strife among the colonists was the realization that a certain amount of subversion was taking place. The Spanish government was learning a good deal about the Jamestown settlement from reports originating within the colony itself. Soon after the *Susan Constant* and the *Godspeed* arrived in England, one Captain Waiman (or Warman) was taken into custody for carrying coded messages from the Jamestown settlement addressed to Philip III of Spain. In Jamestown council member George Kendall, suspected from the start by James Read, the blacksmith, of being a spy in the employ of Philip III, was finally openly accused, convicted, and executed.[19] Even Wingfield, after his recall from the council presidency, was charged with mutinous intentions and was imprisoned on the *Discovery*, the pinnace which had been left at Jamestown. The charge against Wingfield was never proved, however, and he was eventually released.

Conditions in the colony worsened as the summer wore on. Beginning in August there were deaths every few days. On August 6, John Asbie died of "the bloody flux"; three days later George Flowre died of "the swelling." William Bruster died on August 10 from arrow wounds, as did Jeremy Alicock four days

[18] Abbot, *A Virginia Chronology, 1585–1783*, 3–4.

[19] An account of Waiman's espionage for Spain may be found in Alexander Brown, *The Genesis of the United States*, I, 113, which contains the text of a letter from Sir Dudley Carleton in London to John Chamberlain, dated August 18, 1607. The letter reads, in part: "One Captain Waiman a special favorite of Sir William Copes was taken this weeke in a port in Kent shipping himself for Spaine, with intent it is thought to have betraied his friends and shewed the Spaniards a meanes how to defeat the Virginia attempt."

later. On August 22 the *Discovery's* guns announced the death of Captain Bartholomew Gosnold.[20] By the end of summer, the colony's population had been reduced by half.

Percy recorded the distress of the colonists:

> There were never Englishmen left in a forreigne Countrey in such miserie as wee were in this new discovered Virginia. Wee watched every three nights lying on the bare cold ground . . . which brought our men to bee most feeble wretches, our food was but a small can of Barlie sod in water to five men a day, our drinke cold water taken out of the River, which was at floud verie Salt, at a low tide full of slime and filth, which was the destruction of many of our men. Thus we lived for the Space of five moneths in this miserable distresse, not having five able men to man . . . [our] Bulwarkes upon any occasion. If it had not pleased God to have put terror in the Savage hearts, we had all perished by those wild and cruell Pagans, being in weakened estate as we were.[21]

Because of her regular visits to Jamestown, Pocahontas was inevitably aware of the destitution of the colonists and of the decimation of their numbers from disease. It was at this time that she began her ministrations to them, repaying the kindness and attention shown to her by John Smith and others. In September she persuaded some of her people to bring half-ripe corn to the fort. She was unquestionably responsible for directing Smith to those Powhatans who were less unfriendly than others and might give some assistance to the colony. Her half-brother Pochins supplied Smith with maize and fish. The Quiyoughcohanocks gave him maize and wild game.

[20] Smith, *Generall Historie*, Book III, 43–44; Purchas, *Purchas His Pilgrimes*, IV, 1691. Captain Bartholomew Gosnold (or Gosnoll), who brought the *Godspeed* to the New World, was Newport's second-in-command. He remained in Jamestown to serve as a member of the council.

[21] Purchas, *Purchas His Pilgrimes*, IV, 1690.

In his later writings, Smith referred to Pocahontas' efforts on behalf of the colonists in those difficult times and in subsequent years. Writing to Queen Anne in 1616, he declared that "[Pocahontas] was . . . the instrument to prusurve this colonie from death, famine, and utter confusion."[22]

22 Smith, *Generall Historie*, Book IV, 122.

CHAPTER V

The Rescue

BESIDES BRINGING FOOD TO THE COLONISTS and directing John Smith to more or less hospitable areas within the Powhatan Confederacy, Pocahontas performed yet another important service for the colonists, the act for which she has been immortalized in history. Her rescue of John Smith from a ritualistic Powhatan execution kept alive the hope of Powhatan-English co-operation and served to strengthen the colonists' morale.

Early in December, 1607, Smith decided to venture into the Chickahominy River country to procure corn from the inhabitants, who were presumably more or less hospitable, and also to explore the Chickahominy to its headwaters in hopes of discovering a great lake that would open into the "Indian Sea," a discovery greatly desired by the English. With Smith on the expedition were seven other colonists, among them John Robinson, George Cassen, and Thomas Emry.

Leaving Jamestown around December 10 in a shallop, Smith's party traveled up the river to the present Windsor Shades, at which point the river narrows into a shallow stream. Smith decided to leave the shallop there, guarded by four members of the party, whom he cautioned not to wander into the woods and run the risk of encountering hostile Indians. Then Smith, Emry, and Robinson continued upstream in a small dugout canoe manned by two seemingly peaceful Powhatans whom the party had met after leaving Jamestown and who had agreed to guide Smith on a "fowling expedition."

Upon reaching Bottom Bridge, near the present Providence Forge, Smith and one of the Powhatan guides left the canoe and set out on foot to explore the nearby countryside, leaving Robinson, Emry, and the second guide to make camp. A quarter of an hour later, when he was in the vicinity of White Oak Swamp, Smith heard a savage yell. Seizing his guide and using him as a shield, Smith whipped out his pistol and held it against the guide's back, threatening to kill the Indian if anything happened to Robinson and Emry. At that moment, an arrow shot from a nearby thicket grazed Smith's thigh, and in the distance he saw two Indians with drawn bows pointed in his direction. Quickly Smith fired at the Indians, missing both. Reloading the pistol, a French wheel lock, he succeeded in killing three or four bowmen who sprang from the woods. Before he could escape, however, a much larger number of Powhatans appeared and surrounded him.

After closing in on Smith and his guide, the Powhatan bowmen threw down their weapons and waited for Smith to discard his own arms. However, having been instructed by His Majesty as were all the colonists—never to abandon weapons in the presence of savages, Smith ignored the invitation. Using his limited Powhatan vocabulary, he was finally able to learn that George Cassen had wandered away from the shallop and had been killed after divulging Smith's whereabouts.[1] Robinson and Emry, surprised by the Indians while making camp, had also been killed, Emry's body having been pierced by more than twenty arrows.

Smith gathered that he, being a captain, was to be spared the fate of his fellow colonists. Yet he realized that there would be a final reckoning for him, too, and he decided to try to retreat to the shallop. Pistol in hand, he began backing away from his captors toward the campsite, but he had not gone far when he slipped off the edge of an embankment into an icy bog, taking the guide with him. There the two remained hopelessly caught until "being near dead with cold he [Smith] threw away his arms."[2]

The Indians pulled him and his guide from the bog and conducted them to the campsite. There, before the campfire kindled by Robinson and Emry, Smith's captors chafed his numbed legs until circulation was restored. Then, obeying his demands to be presented to their werowance, they brought him before one of Pocahontas' more warlike uncles, Opechancanough.[3]

---

[1] The aftermath of Cassen's capture was not pleasant. He was tied to a tree and brutally mutilated, his fingers, hands, and legs hacked off with the Powhatans' torture weapons, mussel shells and reeds rendered razor sharp by much honing on rock or flint. Thrown into a nearby fire, the members were yet burning when Cassen, still alive, was disemboweled, and his remains were burned with the tree.

[2] Smith, *Generall Historie*, Book III, 46.

[3] Smith and other colonists had given the title King of Pamunkey to Opechancanough, after encountering him at the Weanocs' village seven months earlier.

Smith, though weaponless, was not lacking in resourcefulness. He presented to Opechancanough an ivory compass he was carrying, hoping to divert the chief and gain his good will. The tactic proved to be a clever one, as Smith's account of the episode reveals:

> . . . Much they marvailed at the playing of the Fly and Needle, which they could see so plainly and yet not touch it, because of the glass that covered them. But when he [Smith] demonstrated by that Globelike jewell the roundness of the earth, and skies, the spheare of the sunne, moone, and starrs, and how the sun did chase the night round about the world continually; the greatness of the Land and Sea, the diversitie of nations, varietie of complexions, and how we were to them Antipodes, and many other such like matters, they all stood as amazed with admiration. Not withstanding, within an hour after they tyed him to a tree, and as many as could stand about him prepared to shoot him, but the King holding up the compass in his hand, they all laid down their bows and arrows, and in a triumphant manner led him to Orapaks.[4]

Smith described the six-mile march to Orapaks, a Powhatan hunting preserve: ". . . drawing themselves all in fyle, the King in the midst had all their Peeces and Swords bore before him. Captain Smith was led after him by three great Savages holding him fast by each arme: and on each side six went in fyle with their Arrows nocked."[5]

Arriving at Orapaks, situated between the upper Chickahominy and Pamunkey rivers, Smith saw thirty or forty temporary shelters[6] from which streamed a large number of women and

---

[4] Smith, *Generall Historie*, Book III, 47.

[5] *Ibid.*

[6] The women of the tribe made the temporary hunting shelters by bending saplings into the shapes of beehives and covering the frameworks with removable mats. At the end of a hunt they dismantled and rolled up the shelters and carried them on their backs to another location.

children to stare at him as he was led to Powhatan's lodge, Rasa-wrack, about a mile from Orapaks. There Smith was encircled by Opechancanough's screeching warriors, who danced about him three times[7] and then led him into the lodge, which was some "fiftie or sixtie yards in length." There he was kept under guard by forty or fifty "tall fellows." Later his guards brought him venison and bread, which he could not eat, his stomach being at that time "not very good." The food that he could not eat "they put in baskets and tied over his head. About midnight they set the meate again before him, all this time not one of them would eat a bit with him, till the next morning they brought him as much more."[8]

While Smith was imprisoned in the lodge, the father of a young Powhatan whom Smith had wounded earlier in the day tried to kill him but was stopped by one of the guards. Smith was taken to see the dying youth, and, aware of the Powhatans' superstitions and their belief in wizardry, he promised to restore the youth's health if his captors would let him go to Jamestown for a vial of curative water. The Powhatans refused his offer and instead made one of their own. They offered Smith "life, liberty, land, and women"[9] if he would betray his fellow colonists by advising the Powhatans on how best to make an attack on the Jamestown fort. Smith, of course, refused the offer.

---

[7] The dance, composed of frenzied gyrations, was already familiar to Smith, who had seen similar dancing outside the Jamestown fort. He described the dancers thus: "Everyone his quiver of Arrows, and at his backe a club; on his arme a Fox or an Otter's skin, or some such matter for his vambrace; their heads and shoulders painted red . . . made an exceeding handsome show . . . with Bow in his hand, and with the skinne of [a] Bird with her wings abroad dried, tyed on his head, a peece of copper, a white shell, a long feather, with a small rattle growing at the tayles of their snakes tyed to it, or some such toy." (*Generall Historie*, Book III, 47.)

[8] *Ibid.*

[9] *Ibid.*

Finally, after several days had passed,[10] the Powhatans decided to exhibit Smith to the inhabitants of the region that, in 1604, had been visited by the white man who on his kidnapping expedition had killed the werowance of Rappahannock. The Powhatans were eager to know whether Smith was the same person.

Around December 18 he was taken from Orapaks and conducted by water and over land to Menapucunt (Menapacant),[11] and then to other towns and villages of the Pamunkeys. Then he was exhibited among the Youghtanunds, a tribe living in what is today King William County. He was also taken to the region of the Piankatanks, on the north side of the Piankatank River in Middlesex County. And he was taken to Rappahannock, on the north side of the Rappahannock River in Richmond County.

It was at Rappahannock that Smith's "exhibition" took its most serious turn. He sensed that his life depended on whether or not the Rappahannock tribe identified him as the slayer of their werowance. Fortunately, Smith was a short man, and the

[10] During this confinement Smith made claim to another kind of wizardry: "In part of a Table booke he [Smith] writ his minde to them at the Fort what was intended . . . and without fayle send him such things as he writ for." Inducing the Indians to deliver the note, he told them about the great guns and machines that they would encounter upon their arrival at the Fort. "Yet they went to Jamestown in as bitter weather as could be of frost and snow, and within three days returned with an answer." (*Ibid.*) To Smith's captors the answer was proof that the note he had written could speak, and they were convinced that he possessed occult powers akin to those of their own priests.

[11] The Pamunkey tribe, the largest single tribe in the Powhatan Confederacy, occupied the land around the junction of the Mattaponi and Pamunkey rivers, in present King William County. The Pamunkeys were ruled by Pocahontas' three uncles, Opechancanough, Kecatough, and Opitchapan. Called the "triumvirate" by the English, the three werowances ruled with powers second only to Powhatan's and were in turn to succeed Powhatan as rulers of the confederacy. Opechancanough's residence, Menapucunt (or Menapacant), was above the present West Point. Kecatough's residence was at nearby Cinquoteck, at West Point. Opitchapan's province was further upstream on the Mattaponi and upper Pamunkey rivers.

Rappahannocks remembered that the slayer had been much taller. Smith was exonerated of the 1604 crime.

However, the Powhatans were not yet ready to free him. They kept him prisoner in hope that he would provide information about Jamestown and its form. The final decision about his fate was apparently to rest with the great Chief Powhatan himself at Werowocomoco. Returned to Menapucunt about December 25, Smith was hurried off to Uttamussack to be interrogated in one of Powhatan's royal residences.

About December 29, after being thoroughly prepared by Powhatan's head priest in an elaborate ritual[12] designed to ascertain whether or not he "intended them well," Smith was taken to Werowocomoco, by dugout canoe in bitter, damp winter weather. Upon his arrival he was greeted by two hundred grim "Courtiers," staring at him "as [though] he had been a monster."[13] He was brought before the great Powhatan as the chief

[12] According to Smith, his guards seated him on a mat before a fire in the house temple and left, whereupon there "came skipping in a great grim fellow, all painted over with coale mingled with oyle; and many Snakes and Weasel's skins stuffed with moss, and all their tayles tied together, so as they met on the crowne of his head in a tassel; and round about the tassel was a Coronet of feathers." Powhatan's head priest then danced around the fire, uttering strange invocations, to the accompaniment of a rattle. Next he sprinkled corn meal around the fire after which he was joined by "three more such like devils," who sang and danced and then were joined by three more dancers, all of whom "with their rattles began a song, which ended, the chief priest layd down five wheat cornes: then strayning his arms with such violence that he sweat and his veins swelled, he began a short Oration,: at the conclusion they all gave a short groan; and then layd down three grains more. After that they began their song again, and then another Oration, laying doune so many cornes as before, till they had twice incircled the fire; that done, they took a bunch of little sticks prepared for that purpose. . . . and at the end of every song and Oration they laid down a stick between the divisions of the corn." The ritual, Smith learned, was highly symbolic. "The circle of meal signified their country, the circles of corn the bounds of the sea, and the sticks his [Smith's] country. They imagined the world to be round, like a trencher, and they in the midst." (*Generall Historie*, Book III, 48.)

[13] *Ibid.*, 49.

sat majestically before a fire inside his dwelling "upon a seat like a bedstead, . . . covered with a great robe, made of rarowcun [raccoon] skins, and all the tayles hanging by."[14] The chief was surrounded by a large number of Powhatans. Seated on either side of him was a young woman "of 16 or 18 years, and along on each side [of the room] two rows of men, and behind them as many women, with all their heads bedecked with the white down of birds."[15]

Smith was the first of the Jamestown colonists to lay eyes on Pocahontas' father and the first to penetrate, albeit unwillingly, into the very heart of Powhatan society and culture. As for the Powhatans, Smith was the first of the Jamestown settlers to enter their midst. Upon Smith's entrance into the royal presence, a shout went up among the people, and Queen Oppussoquionuske, the werowance of Apamatuks and Pocahontas' aunt, brought Smith water in which to wash his hands, after which he was brought "a bunch of feathers instead of towel to dry them."[16] Then followed a great feast—venison, bread made from maize, a stew made with corn, and wild turkey poults—in preparation for the disposition of Smith that was to follow. For it was clear that Smith was to be put to death.

When the feast ended, Powhatan and his advisers held a lengthy parley, after which "two great stones were brought before Powhatan: then as many as could laid hands on him [Smith], dragged him to [the stones] and thereon laid his head." The execution was to be the evening's entertainment—and was to rid Chief Powhatan not merely of a white man but of an especially clever and industrious white man who had had the audacity to venture deep into Powhatan territory and to ask the

14 *Ibid.*
15 *Ibid.*
16 *Ibid.*

Powhatans to aid the English, the people Chief Powhatan most despised and feared.

But the father had not reckoned on his compassionate daughter. As the Powhatan warriors were about to fall on Smith with their clubs, the young princess, doubtless out of gratitude to Smith for his kindness to her, stepped from the crowd of Powhatans who had come to witness the execution. Quickly she took Smith's "head in her armes and laid her owne upon his to save him from death."[17]

Powhatan responded to the impulsive action of his favorite daughter and ordered Smith spared. The captive was brought "to a great house in the woods," where he was seated on a mat before a fire and left alone for a time. But "not long after from behind a mat that divided the house, was made the dolefulest noise he ever heard; then Powhatan more like a devil than a man with some two hundred more as black as himself, came unto him [Smith] and told him now they were friends and presently he should go to Jamestown to send him two great guns and a grind-stone for which he would give him the country of Capahowosick [Capahowasic] and forever esteem him as his son Nantaquoud!"[18]

Obviously Chief Powhatan had discovered an advantage to himself in sparing Smith's life and bringing him into the Powhatan fold. Powhatan's announcement of the "adoption" coupled with the request for guns was a transparent piece of political

---

[17] *Ibid.* Strangely enough, Smith did not immediately publicize the story of his rescue by Pocahontas. His failure to include this dramatic episode in his first published accounts of his capture and imprisonment by the Powhatans has never been explained. Smith's English publishers, fearful that his story of near death might discourage other colonists from going to Virginia, may have deleted the event from Smith's narrative. Or Smith himself omitted the story. The account of his rescue was not published until 1624, when it appeared in the *Generall Historie*, Book III, 46–49.

[18] *Ibid.*

strategy. Smith agreed to the proposal, and the adoption ceremony took place two days later at Werowocomoco, after which
Smith was sent on his way back to Jamestown, accompanied by
twelve Powhatan guides.[19]

Smith and his escort arrived at Jamestown early on the morning of January 2, 1608. Smith, again relying on his store of wit
and ingenuity to satisfy Powhatan's demand for weapons, offered to give Rawhunt, Powhatan's chief representative, two
demiculverins and a millstone to take back to Powhatan. Each
of the demiculverins weighed between 3,000 and 4,500 pounds,
and, of course, Rawhunt and his companions could not move
them. Then Smith demonstrated the power of the demiculverins:
"When they did see him discharge them, being loaded with
stones, among the boughs of a great tree loaded with icicles, the
ice and branches came so tumbling down that the poor savages
ran away half dead with fear. But at last we regained some conference with them and gave them such toys: and sent Powhatan,
his women, and children such presents as gave them in general
full content."[20]

So ended Smith's capture, trial, rescue, and adoption—a series
of events that marked the beginning of an even closer relationship between Pocahontas and the English settlers. According to
Powhatan custom, Pocahontas was now Smith's guardian. Like
any other captive turned over to the custody of a female, Smith
had become her special ward or possession. As a result, Pocahontas would play an even greater role in maintaining communication with the colonists in general and with Smith in
particular, and in achieving liaison between her father, who had
not yet abandoned his intention to rid himself of the English,
and the colonists, who were equally determined to remain in the
New World. Pocahontas was to remain a ministrant to the col-

19 *Ibid.*
20 *Ibid.*

ony, but now her activities would be expanded. She was to become much more openly a negotiator recognized by both sides, each using her talents and energies to bargain with the other.

CHAPTER VI

Negotiations

ON THE EVENING OF Saturday, January 2, 1608—the same day
Smith returned to Jamestown—the *Susan Constant*, under the
command of Captain Newport, dropped anchor at the Jamestown waterfront.[1] Earlier in the day Pocahontas and her retinue
of attendants had brought provisions to Jamestown, and she may
well have been on hand to watch the debarkation of nearly one
hundred new colonists, as well as the unloading of long-awaited
supplies and provisions for the Jamestown survivors, whose

[1] Abbot, *A Virginia Chronology, 1585–1783*, 4.

74

number had dwindled to scarcely more than thirty. Among the supplies Newport had brought were trade goods for the Indians.

Pocahontas may also have witnessed Newport's immediate intervention in a crisis that had arisen during the day between Smith on the one hand and John Ratcliffe (the new president of the council), Gabriel Archer, and Captain John Martin on the other. Ratcliffe, Archer, and Martin had seriously questioned Smith's story about his sojourn among the Powhatans[2] and had accused him of being responsible for the deaths of Emry and Robinson. His accusers had arranged a hasty trial. Archer, the prosecutor, who had studied law at Gray's Inn, based his case on the Levitical law. Ratcliffe, the civil authority of the colony, pronounced Smith guilty and condemned him to death by hanging. The noose had actually been placed around Smith's neck when Newport's booming cannon salute from the waterfront stayed the execution. After Newport came ashore and learned of the situation, he persuaded the council members to let Smith go free, reminding them of the services Smith had performed for the colony.

Upon seeing the arrival of the new colonists, Pocahontas must have been aware of the inevitable difficulties they would face because of her father's enmity. At Werowocomoco, Smith had implied that the colonists would soon depart from Powhatan shores. A question Powhatan had repeatedly asked Smith was why the English had settled at Jamestown in the first place. Smith's temporizing answer was that they had merely sought refuge at Jamestown because they were being pursued by the Spaniards and that the colonists would depart when Newport came back. Then Powhatan would ask why the English did not leave on their pinnace, to which Smith would reply that the *Discovery* leaked and could not be used by the colonists until it was repaired. Powhatan had naturally concluded that the English

2 *Ibid.*

would depart as soon as some means of transportation presented itself. Now the *Susan Constant* had arrived with more colonists and fresh provisions.

The arrival of the new colonists undoubtedy boded further trouble with the Powhatans, and an event that occurred a week later placed the colonists in an even more precarious position. On January 7 a fire broke out at Jamestown, destroying a good part of the fort, the colonists' thatched huts and their crude little church—along with Mr. Hunt's cherished theological library—and, most disastrously, the roof of the storehouse and most of the food supplies that Newport had just brought from England. Once again the English were in the difficult position of needing help from Indians who had expected to witness their departure.

Pocahontas responded to the situation: "Now ever[y] once in four or five days Pocahontas and her attendants brought . . . so much provision that saved many of their lives."[3] Pocahontas presented the provisions not only to Smith but also to Captain Newport, for in his conversations with Powhatan, Smith had referred to the captain as "Father Newport" to indicate his important position. Acting now not simply as a friend of the colonists but also as a representative of her father, Pocahontas included Newport in her special attention, realizing that, since he had been influential in saving Smith from hanging, the Powhatans might profitably negotiate with him.

As far as the Powhatans were concerned, their primary interest in negotiation lay in bartering advantageously to acquire as many English goods as possible. Such negotiation was indicative of a change in the Indians' policy. Chief Powhatan had decided that the most effective means of eliminating the English was to acquire the materials and weapons that the English used. By his orders the colonists' near neighbors, the Quiyoughcohanocks, Paspaheghs, Weanocs, and Chickahominies, no longer attacked

[3] Smith, *Generall Historie*, Book III, 49.

every colonist they encountered outside the fort; instead they began visiting the colony, bartering for trade goods and bartering with greater expertise than heretofore. To Smith's disgust, Newport's mariners traded the Indians one pound of copper for Indian produce that before Newport's arrival in January could have been bought for one ounce of the metal.

Most significantly, Chief Powhatan sent word by Pocahontas that he would like "Father Newport" to visit him at Werowocomoco. Late in February, after the rebuilding of the fire-damaged fort and repairs to the palisades enclosing it, Smith and Newport, with a bodyguard of thirty or forty colonists, journeyed to Werowocomoco, sailing the *Discovery* down the James River to Kecoughtan, rounding the tip of the peninsula, and, directed by their compasses, sailing twenty miles or more up the Pamunkey River to Poetan Bay.[4]

Though Chief Powhatan had asked specifically to see Newport, as the chief's adopted son, Smith took charge of the visit. He left Newport in the pinnace with a bodyguard, while he and eighteen other colonists went ashore in small boats to prepare for the meeting. Pocahontas had already informed Powhatan of the impending visit, and an escort of some two hundred warriors met Smith when he landed at Poetan Bay, conducting him and the other colonists over a series of primitive bridges to Powhatan's lodge at Werowocomoco. At the lodge Smith noted that "more than fortie platters of fine bread stood . . . in two files on each side of the doore. Four or five hundred people made a guard behind them for our passage: and Proclamation was made, none upon pain of death to presume to doe us any wrong of discourtesie."[5]

Chief Powhatan received his visitors in full ceremonial dress

---

[4] Smith made mental notes of the water route to Werowocomoco so that he could reproduce it accurately on the map he planned to make of the Powhatan country.

[5] Smith, *Generall Historie*, Book III, 51.

and "strained himselfe to the utmost of his greatnesse to entertaine them with great shouts of joy, Orations of protestation; and
with the most plenty of victualls he could provide."⁶ Smith, in
turn, presented to Powhatan "a suit of red woolen cloth, a white
greyhound, and a sugar loaf hat such as King James himself
wore."⁷ The white greyhound was a special novelty for Powhatan, and all the gifts were appropriately acknowledged, though
not by the great Powhatan himself but by three minor werowances. With many gestures, grimaces, and flowery orations the
chiefs assured Smith of Powhatan's friendship and of his willingness to provide the colonists with corn until they could harvest
their crops.

Then Powhatan himself entered the conversation, asking
Smith about the cannon and the grindstone that had been promised earlier. Smith explained that he had offered Rawhunt and
the other Powhatans four demiculverins but that they had refused them. Powhatan laughed, acknowledging that the demiculverins had been too heavy to transport and added that he
would be willing to accept a smaller cannon.

Next Powhatan asked Smith and the other Englishmen to put
aside their guns and other arms while they were in his house.
He pointed out that the walls of the house were hung with the
Powhatan bows, arrows, and other war weapons. Why should the
English not also lay down their arms in Powhatan's presence?
Smith replied that laying down their arms "was a ceremony
our enemies desired, never our friends."⁸ Quickly changing the
subject, Smith assured Powhatan that the colonists and their
guns would be ready to serve Powhatan in any future wars he
might wage against his Siouan enemies the Monacans and the
Manahoacs.

⁶ *Ibid.*, 51–52.
⁷ Barbour, *The Three Worlds of Captain John Smith*, 178.
⁸ *Ibid.*, 179.

Smith and the eighteen men who had accompanied him spent the night in Powhatan's lodge. The next day Captain Newport came ashore and was duly presented to Chief Powhatan. As a gesture of good will, Newport had brought along a young English boy named Thomas Savage,[9] whom he proposed to "loan" to the Powhatans so that the boy might learn their language and eventually act as an interpreter between the two peoples. Powhatan was impressed by this act and insisted that Newport accept in exchange a young Powhatan boy named Namontack, who could in turn learn the colonists' language—and could even go back to England with Newport when next he sailed. After the exchange of "sons," Powhatan climaxed the ceremony by bestowing upon each of his visitors a large basket filled to overflowing with dried beans.

Newport invited Chief Powhatan to come aboard the *Discovery* and examine the trade goods that he had brought along to barter, but Powhatan made it clear that he had no intention of boarding the pinnace; the trade goods would have to be brought ashore. "It is not agreeable to my greatness," Powhatan said haughtily, "in this trifling manner to trade for trifles; and I esteeme you also a great werowance. Therefore lay me downe all your commodities together; what I like I will take, and in recompense give you what I think fitting their value."[10]

The store of copper kettles, hatchets, knives, scissors, and blue glass beads were brought from the pinnace and spread before Powhatan in his long house, whereupon Powhatan estimated their value in corn and other provisions in Powhatan's storehouse.

To Smith's dismay, Newport agreed to exchange twelve great copper kettles for the same amount of corn that Powhatan had

[9] Powhatan was confused about Thomas Savage's name and called the boy Thomas Newport.

[10] Smith, *Generall Historie*, Book III, 52.

earlier bartered to Smith for one small kettle. To compensate for Powhatan's inflated valuation of the corn, Smith began extolling the virtues of the glass beads, telling Powhatan that blue beads were very rare, being the color of the sky, and that they were not to be worn by any but the greatest kings. According to Anas Todkill, a member of the party, Smith was so convincing in his praise of the beads that Powhatan was "halfe madde to be the owner of such strange Jewells; so ere we departed, for a pound or two of blue beads Powhatan paid Newport and Smith two or three hundred bushels of corn, Yet parted good friends."[11]

After his visit with Powhatan, Newport felt that he had ingratiated himself quite satisfactorily with the Indians and was inclined to pursue a more liberal policy toward them. Later, when Powhatan sent twenty turkeys to the colonists, Newport complied with Powhatan's request for twenty English swords in return. On April 20, 1608, feeling confident that relations between the Powhatans and the colonists were cordial, Newport sailed for England in the *Susan Constant.*[12]

For his part, Smith had been dismayed by Newport's liberality with the Powhatans. Now once again the colony's chief representative to the Indians, he decided to return to a harder line. When Powhatan sent another twenty turkeys and demanded again an equal number of swords, Smith refused to make the exchange. Then Powhatan undertook to procure the swords by

[11] *Ibid.* After leaving Powhatan, Smith and Newport also visited Opechancanough and the other brothers. On those occasions Smith also bartered the blue glass beads. "None durst wear them," Smith told Opechancanough, "but their great kings, their wives, and children." So impressed was Opechancanough that he, too, paid extravagantly in corn for the beads.

[12] Wingfield, the deposed president of the local council at Jamestown, sailed with Newport. In reporting on activities in the Jamestown colony, Wingfield failed to mention the part that Smith had played in the procurement of provisions from the Indians, probably because it had been Smith, together with Ratcliffe, Martin, and Archer, who had brought about Wingfield's removal from office and his subsequent imprisonment on the *Discovery.*

stealth. "He caused his people with twentie devices to obtaine them," Anas Todkill later reported. "At last by ambuscadoes at our very ports . . . Powhatan's warriors would take them perforce, surprise us at worke or anyway."[13] These acts infuriated Smith, who "without further deliberation gave them such an encounter that this thievery of swords came to an end."[14]

Suppression of the thievery brought on new difficulties with the Indians. "Some he [Smith] so terrified with whipping, beating, and imprisonment" that the Indians sought revenge and threatened the fort gates in an effort to force Smith to give up seven Powhatan prisoners he had captured. If the prisoners were not released, the Powhatans warned the colonists "were all but dead men."[15] Smith refused to give up the prisoners and ordered "several vollies of shot" fired inside the fort to make the Indians think one of the captives had been executed.

The Indians retreated, but for a time barter ceased, and now that Newport had left, Powhatan's plan to acquire English weapons was being foiled. It was clear that new negotiations must be arranged. Once again Pocahontas was called upon to mediate between Smith and her father—two equally temperamental, clever, and stubborn men.

Early in May, 1608, Pocahontas came to Jamestown as her father's emissary, bringing presents for the colonists, whose number had once again been augmented by the arrival of forty new colonists in the *Phoenix*, under the command of Captain Francis Nelson. Pocahontas had come to negotiate the release of the seven Indians imprisoned in the fort. She begged Smith to "excuse him [Powhatan] of the injuries done by some rash and untoward captaines [warriors], desiring their liberties this time, with the assurance of his love."[16] Smith pondered the matter and

13 Smith, *Generall Historie*, Book III, 54.
14 *Ibid.*   15 *Ibid.*
16 *Ibid.*

then "corrected" the prisoners and released them to Pocahontas, "for whose sake onely," reported Todkill, "he fayned to have saved their lives."[17]

Pocahontas' intervention restored peace, at least for the time being, and brought to the Jamestown colonists the first really calm days they had had since their arrival twelve months before. Food was plentiful, the fort was in good condition, and new colonists had arrived. The Englishmen could venture outside the palisades with less fear of being attacked. Harsh winter weather had given way to spring. The colonists were busy planting gardens, fishing, and searching for gold and other precious metals in the Virginia soil.[18]

Spring and summer passed. Pocahontas continued her ambassadorial work, bearing messages and bringing provisions to Jamestown. In the autumn Pocahontas, now eleven or twelve years old, at an age when Powhatan girls were "shamefacd to be seene bare,"[19] began to appear dressed in a short, apron-like skirt of buckskin fringed at the lower edge, modestly folding her arms across her breasts when she was in the presence of strangers, and frequently repeating, as did the Indian girls who accompanied her, the English phrase she had learned: "Love

[17] *Ibid.*

[18] From the time of their arrival in Jamestown the colonists had had great hopes of finding gold. Smith felt that too much attention was given to searching for the "gilded durt." Others, such as Captain John Martin, the son of a London goldsmith, was much more enthusiastic about the possibility, and under his direction the hold of the *Phoenix* was loaded with dirt—rather than cedar, as Smith wished—to be taken to London for assay. Martin's departure for London did not displease Smith or Todkill, who commented, "Captain Martin being always very sickly and unserviceable, and desirous to injoy the credit of his supposed act of finding the golden mine, was most willingly admitted to return for England." (*Ibid.*)

[19] Strachey, *Historie*, Cap. V, 65.

you not me? Love you not me?"[20] Pocahontas was coming of age, and although she had already played an important part in James-town's settlement, she was soon to play an even more complex and difficult role.

[20] Smith, *Generall Historie*, Book III, 67.

CHAPTER VII

Powhatan's Coronation

In the autumn of 1608, Pocahontas must have felt that her conciliatory efforts had borne fruit. On September 8, John Smith, her friend and adopted brother, was elected president of the Jamestown council, and a month or so later the colonists staged an event especially designed to please her father. The cordiality was not to endure, but for a span of a few short months in the fall of the year, Pocahontas had reason to be optimistic.

Upon his election Smith made a vigorous effort to ensure the colony's continued progress and to correct some of the weak-

84

nesses of previous administrations. He was especially eager for increased colonization in the Jamestown area. In a series of expeditions during the summer of 1608 through the Chesapeake Bay area,[1] he had found evidence of French "infiltration" as close as the Susquehanna River. There the hospitable seven-foot-tall Susquehannock Indians had shown Smith metal hatchets given to them by Frenchmen from settlements in Canada.[2] Smith was convinced that it was now a matter of urgency for England to establish a truly permanent foothold in the New World, not only to provide wealth for the mother country and relieve the overpopulation at home but also to serve as a symbol of territorial expansion that would impress rival European powers.

With this goal in mind Smith took stock of what needed to be done and put all hands to work:

> The Church was repaired;[3] the Store-house was recovered; buildings prepared for the Supplies we expected; the Fort reduced to five-square forme; the order of the Watch renewed; the squadrons (each setting of the Watch) trained; the whole Company every Saturday exercised, in the plaine by the West Bulwarke, prepared for that purpose . . . where sometimes more than a hundred Salvages

[1] Shortly after Newport's departure for England in April, 1608, Smith and fourteen other colonists set off again to search for the "Indian Sea." On June 16 they entered the Potomac River and traveled upriver to a point beyond present-day Washington, D.C. En route back to Jamestown, at the mouth of the Rappahannock River Smith was attacked by a sting ray while spear fishing and severely wounded in one arm. The injury was treated by Dr. Walter Russell, and the colonists named the site of the accident Stingray Point, the name it still bears today. (Abbot, *A Virginia Chronology, 1585–1783,* 4.)

[2] Smith, *Generall Historie,* Book III, 67.

[3] The church had fallen into disuse after Mr. Hunt's death in July. After it was repaired, Smith described it thus: "[It] was a homely thing like a barne set upon Crachets, covered with rafts, sedge, and earth, so was also the walls: the best of our houses of the like curiosity. . . . Yet wee had daily Common Prayer . . . and surely God did most mercifully heare us." (*Advertisements,* 32.)

85

would stand in amazement to behold, how a file would batter a tree, whereby he [Smith] would make them a mark to shoot at.[4]

On October 8 Captain Newport arrived at Jamestown on the *Mary and Margaret*, bringing seventy new colonists—including the colony's first women, a Mrs. Forest and her maid, Anne Burras. Smith was pleased by the arrivals, but he well knew that additional colonists would make more difficult his task of maintaining peaceful relations with Chief Powhatan. This problem had been anticipated by the Virginia Company, and the method of handling it was not left to Smith's discretion. Upon landing at Jamestown, Newport handed Smith an official packet of orders composed by Virginia Company officers and also by King James.

Though the orders pertained to several matters,[5] the most important one was designed to win over Chief Powhatan to accept the new colonists. Smith and Newport were to arrange to crown Powhatan as king of the Powhatan nation in an elaborate and colorful ceremony at Jamestown. The coronation was to impress Chief Powhatan so deeply that he would approve of the colonists ever after.[6] Reading these instructions, Smith bluntly declared that the august members of the Virginia Company were "fools" and that King James was no better. The whole idea "was gro-

[4] The Powhatan marksmen could hit Smith's metal target, of course, but an arrow shaft would break into splinters and the point would fall to the ground. When the colonists fired their guns at the target, their shot penetrated the metal, thereby proving to the Powhatans the superiority of the colonists' guns—a point Smith wanted to drive home, for the Powhatans' fear of the colonists' weapons was an important part of his program for dealing with the Indians. (Smith, *Generall Historie*, Book III, 66.)

[5] Smith and Newport were directed to make further efforts to find the survivors of the Roanoke colony; to see that the "Poles" and "Dutch-men" sent to Jamestown with Newport began making pitch, tar, glass, and "soape ashes"; to explore the Monacan country above the falls near Richmond; and to continue searching for gold and other minerals. (Smith, *Generall Historie*, Book III, 66–67.)

[6] *Ibid.*

86

tesque enough to have emanated from the teeming brain of James I after a nickle noggin of his native usequehaugh."[7]

Yet the order must be obeyed. For the ceremony Newport had brought from England "a scarlet cloke and apparell, a bason, ewer, bed, and furniture." The ewer, basin, and bed were presents from King James. To furnish the bed there were curtains, canopy, and coverlets made of rich damask lined with buckram —typical furnishings for the beds of English royalty.

While Newport went off to explore the Monacan country in accordance with Virginia Company orders, Smith reluctantly set out for Werowocomoco to arrange for Powhatan's visit to Jamestown. On the fifteen-mile journey he was accompanied by Andrew Buckler, Captain Richard Waldo, Samuel Collier, Edward Brinton, and the Indian ward Namontack, who had returned to Jamestown with Newport. Upon his arrival at Powhatan's lodge Smith was told that the chief was about thirty miles away. A runner was sent to inform Powhatan about his visitors.

Meanwhile, Pocahontas, who had remained at Werowocomoco, provided entertainment for Smith and his companions. The entertainment, which Smith later called "A Virginia Mask," was apparently both pleasurable and shocking. He and his companions were conducted by Pocahontas and her attendants to "a fayre plaine field" and seated on mats before a fire, around which were gathered a goodly number of Powhatan men, women, and children. Suddenly "amongst the woods was heard such a hydeous noise and shreeking, that the English betooke themselves to their armes and seized on two or three old men by them, supposing Powhatan with all his power was come to surprise them."[8]

But the Englishmen's fears were soon allayed by Pocahontas, who, with one hand over her heart and the other raised skyward,

[7] John Fiske, *Old Virginia and Her Neighbors*, I, 133.
[8] Smith, *Generall Historie*, Book III, 67.

willed Smith "to kill her if any hurt was intended." The Powhatans seated near him also assured him that he had nothing to
fear.

Then the colonists were diverted by a brief drama:

> . . . thirtie young women came naked out of the woods, onely cov-
> ered behind and before with a few greene leaves, their bodies all
> painted, some of one colour, some of another, but all differing, their
> leader had a fayre payre of Bucks hornes on her head, and an Otter's
> skinne at her girtle, and another at her arme, a quiver of arrowes at
> her backe, a bow and arrowes in her hand; the next had in her hand
> a Sword, another a club, another a pot-sticke; all horned alike: the
> rest everyone with their severall devises. These fiends with most
> hellish shouts and cryes, rushing from among the trees cast them-
> selves in a ring around the fire, singing and dauncing with most ex-
> cellent ill varietie, of falling into their infernal passions, and
> solemnly againe to sing and daunce; having spent neare an houre
> in this mascarado, as they entered in like manner they departed.
>
> Having reaccomodated themselves, they solemnly invited him
> [Smith] to their lodgings, where he was no sooner within the house,
> but all these Nymphes more tormented him then ever, with crowd-
> ing, pressing, and hanging about him, most tediously crying, Love
> you not me? Love you not me?
>
> This salutation ending, the feast was set, consisting of all the
> Salvage dainties they could devise: some attending, others singing
> and dauncing about him . . . this . . . being ended, with firebrands
> instead of Torches, they conducted him to his lodging.[9]

Pocahontas' entertainment, though evidently embarrassing to
the Englishmen, was a genuine gesture of good will. Just as
Pocahontas had shared provisions with the English, now she
shared with them a ritualistic celebration that expressed in its
unique way both the passion and the dignity of life. Pocahontas,

[9] *Ibid.*

the girl becoming woman, drew from the cultural storehouse of her people a display of their capacity for self-expression.

The next day Powhatan returned to Werowocomoco, and Smith relayed the news of the forthcoming coronation. Using both Thomas Savage and Namontack as interpreters, Smith described the ceremony to the chief and invited him to come to Jamestown for the event. However, Powhatan was well aware of his royal prerogatives. He replied that "if your King have sent me presents, I also am a King and this is my land: Eight dayes will I stay to receive them. Your Father [Newport] is to come to me, not I to him, nor yet to your Fort, neither will I bite at such a bait. . . ."[10] Even when Pocahontas added her pleas to Smith's, Powhatan stubbornly refused to go to Jamestown. All Smith could do was return to the settlement and make arrangements with Newport to hold the ceremony at Werowocomoco.

A few days later Newport, Smith, other members of the council and "fiftie good shot" set out overland on the journey to Werowocomoco. They had dispatched Powhatan's copper crown, the bed, and other presents from King James by boat. When the boat reached Werowocomoco after a circuitous eighty-mile voyage, the presents were brought ashore. With much ado the canopy bed was set up in Powhatan's long house. Then the chief was persuaded to don the fine scarlet cloak. Newport wore full-dress sea captain's regalia. Smith and the other council members wore their Sabbath best.

Powhatan was then instructed to bend his knee and incline his head to receive the copper crown, but at this request Powhatan balked; never in his life had he bent knee or head to anyone. Offshore, the boat's gunners awaited a signal from Newport to fire the cannons at the close of the coronation ceremony. Powhatan's refusal to bend and bow delayed the signal, and, try as they would, none of the English could overcome Powhatan's

[10] *Ibid.*, 68.

resistance. Demonstrations, persuasion, and explanations were in vain. Finally, in desperation, someone came up behind Powhatan and pressed so hard on his shoulders that he was compelled to stoop whether he willed it or not, and quickly the crown was popped on his head. Newport fired a pistol to announce to the world that Powhatan was now "king." And the gunners on the boat fired the cannons.

Terrified by the salvos, Powhatan leaped into the air "in horrible fear" that the colonists' king was attacking Werowocomoco with a fleet of ships. But after being assured by Namontack that his fears were groundless, he recovered his dignity and presented to Newport his own buckskin mantle and moccasins, to be taken to the English king.[11]

When the colonists returned to Jamestown, Smith registered his protest against the proceedings in a rude letter addressed to King James and the "Royal Council of Virginia sitting in London":

RIGHT HONOURABLE LORDS AND GENTLEMEN

. . . Expressly to follow your directions [sent] by Captain Newport, though they be performed, I was directly against it . . . . I feare to the hazard of us all; which now is generally confessed when it is too late. . . . I have . . . crowned Powhatan according to your instructions. . . .

For the Coronation of Powhatan by whose advice you sent him such presents, I know not; but this give me leave to tell you, I feare they will be the confusion of us all ere we heare from you againe.[12]

Smith's fears were reasonable ones. Knowing that the colonists

---

[11] Powhatan's buckskin mantle is on exhibit at the Ashmolean Museum, Oxford University. The mantle is large enough to fit a broad-shouldered man six feet tall or taller. The great number of shells sewed into patterns on the mantle are indicative of Powhatan's enormous wealth at the time of his coronation.

[12] Smith, *Generall Historie*, Book III, 70–72.

were not yet self-sufficient (the storehouses could be filled with grain one month and empty the next) and were therefore dependent upon the Powhatans for much of their food, he felt that by being too generous the English would simply be placing the Indians in a stronger position to hinder the colony's development. Smith's attitude was much more aggressive; he believed in impressing upon the Indian the power and might of the English. In his view, displays of firepower were more effective than gifts of scarlet cloaks and copper crowns.

Unfortunately, Smith's fears proved well founded. The newly crowned king of the Powhatan Confederacy grew increasingly difficult. His coronation did not so much placate him as elevate him to a new position of power and self-confidence. As the English catered to him, Powhatan's generosity diminished. The price of Powhatan corn went up. Even more ominously, late in 1608, Powhatan forbade Pocahontas—the one really effective link between the Indians and the English—to communicate further with the Jamestown colonists, on penalty of death.[13]

[13] *Ibid.*, Book IV, 77.

CHAPTER VIII

The Contest Quickens

ALTHOUGH COMMANDED BY POWHATAN to sever her relations with the colonists, Pocahontas remained sympathetic to them, helping them in countless ways whenever she encountered them in Powhatan territory. Though her task grew considerably more difficult as the struggle between her father and the colonists moved toward its climax and she no longer openly aided the colonists or served as emissary, nevertheless, on at least two occasions in 1609 she intervened to save English lives.

Newport departed for England in December, 1608, leaving

Smith the task of dealing with the aggrandized Powhatan. Once again it was a difficult time for the colonists, with food shortages their most serious problem. Smith had sent word with Newport that the colony's harvest was not "halfe sufficient for so great a number. As for the . . . Corne Newport promised to provide us from Powhatan, he brought us but fourteene Bushels; and from the Monacans nothing. . . . From your Shipe we had not provision in victuals worth twenty pound, and we are more than two hundred to live upon this: the one halfe sick, the other little better."[1] There were fish in the sea, fowl in the air, and game in the woods, but Smith acknowledged that the colonists were "so weake and ignorant, we cannot much trouble them."[2]

Powhatan predictably took advantage of the situation. Increasingly fearful of the growing numbers of colonists at Jamestown and aware of their vulnerability, he began making a number of threatening moves.

Before Newport's departure Smith, growing desperate for provisions, had sent young Matthew Scrivener to Werowocomoco to trade English goods for corn. But Scrivener's mission had not been successful: "Master Scrivener . . . sent with the barges and pinnace to Werowocomoco . . . found the Salvages more ready to fight than trade," and it was only through the intervention of Namontack that Scrivener was able to acquire even "three or four hogsheads of Corne, and as much Pocones which is a red roote, which then was esteemed as a valuable dye."[3]

No longer interested in bartering and negotiation, Powhatan was once again listening to his priests' prophecies about the tribe that would "arise . . . and give end to his empire."[4] He adopted a suspicious and militant attitude toward the colonists, spying

[1] Smith, *Generall Historie*, Book III, 70–72.
[2] *Ibid.*
[3] *Ibid.*, 70.
[4] Strachey, *Historie*, Cap. VIII, 101–102.

upon them "from . . . [his] own courte down almost to our palisado gates."[5]

Nevertheless, Smith had to obtain food. Just before Christmas, 1608, he set out with two barges for the Nansemonds' country to collect four hundred bushels of corn which the tribe had earlier promised him in exchange for the usual English goods—copper, glass beads, brass, and cloth. But upon reaching the Nansemonds' territory, southeast and east of present Suffolk County on the Nansemond River, Smith learned that Powhatan had commanded them to keep their corn and to prevent the English from coming up the river.

Enraged by the refusal and desperate for food, Smith and his men resorted to violence, setting fire to the first Nansemond house they saw. The Indians fearfully and reluctantly gave Smith half the corn in their storehouse, loading it on the barges before nightfall.[6]

The grain was soon eaten, and again the colony was faced with starvation. In subsequent weeks Smith sent Waldo, Scrivener, and Percy to Powhatan villages in search of more corn. Waldo obtained a little corn from the Appomattocs; Percy and Scrivener "could . . . find nothing."[7]

At this critical time several messengers arrived from Powhatan with the surprising news that if Smith would come to Werowocomoco his boats would be loaded with corn from the royal storehouse. In return Smith was to build for Powhatan an English-style house near Werowocomoco and to give Powhatan "a gryndstone, fifty swords, some peeces [guns], a cock and a hen, with much copper and beads."[8] Though Powhatan was driving a hard bargain, Smith had no choice but to accept. What little

[5] *Ibid.*
[6] Smith, *Generall Historie*, Book III, 73.
[7] *Ibid.*
[8] *Ibid.*

94

grain remained in the Jamestown storehouse was rotting or being devoured at an alarming rate by rats that had arrived on the English ships and had since multiplied by the thousands.

Two barges and the pinnace were provisioned, and Smith selected twenty-seven fellow colonists to go with him by the water route. Fourteen colonists, including four Dutch carpenters, were to make the shorter journey overland so that they could begin construction of the house immediately and thereby more speedily fulfill Powhatan's conditions.[9]

Leaving Matthew Scrivener as acting president in his absence, Smith sailed for Werowocomoco, spending the first night with the Warrasqueocs, a friendly Powhatan tribe living near present Smithfield in the northern part of Isle of Wight County.[10] Tackonekintaco, chief of the Warrasqueocs, gave the colonists as much corn as he could spare and tried to dissuade Smith from going on to Werowocomoco, warning him that Powhatan intended to cut his throat.[11]

Smith disregarded the warning and continued downstream to Kecoughtan, Pochins' province at the mouth of the James. There the weather turned bad. Harsh, cold winds off the bay lashed Kecoughtan with sleet and snow, and Smith was forced to remain with Pochins until the weather cleared. Pochins was much friendlier to the English than his father. During the colonists' stay he provided food and shelter and entertainment. The colonists reported that they were "never more merry, nor fed on more plentie of good Oysters, Fish Flesh, Wild—fowle and good bread."[12] The colonists stayed at Kecoughtan into the new year, until January 6, 1609.

---

[9] *Ibid.*, 73, 74. Smith gives conflicting counts of the total number of colonists who participated in this expedition. At one point he states that forty-six men were involved; later he lists only forty-two.

[10] McCary, *Indians in Seventeenth-Century Virginia*, 7.

[11] Smith, *Generall Historie*, Book III, 74.

[12] *Ibid.*

At last the weather cleared, and the expedition made its way around Point Comfort, the pinnace and barges bobbing like corks on the turbulent waters of the bay, and began the arduous journey up the Pamunkey River. So labored was the passage upriver that Smith and his men were forced to go ashore near the Chiskiacks' villages, where they received a much less cordial reception than the Kecoughtans had given them. The Chiskiacks, apparently acting on orders from Chief Powhatan, displayed if not actual hostility certainly petulance toward the colonists, granting them shelter only after repeated requests and then making stealthy attempts to steal guns and powder from the boats. Smith frequently had to order his men to beat drums and discharge weapons to keep the Indians at a distance. Smith commented that, like most of the other Powhatan tribes, the Chiskiacks were afraid "of the noyse of our drums, of our shrill trumpetts and great ordinaunce."[13]

Smith and his men soon pushed on up the Pamunkey River, arriving at Werowocomoco on January 12, 1609. The river at Poetan Bay was frozen over for about half a mile from shore. One of the barges tried to break through the ice but was stranded on a shelf of mud at ebb tide, and Smith and his men were forced to wade ashore. The colonists took up quarters in an unoccupied shelter near the shore and then sent a messenger into Werowocomoco to tell Powhatan of their arrival. Powhatan sent back venison, turkey, and bread and on the following day granted Smith an audience.

Pocahontas was present at the meeting between her father and Smith[14] and was apparently privy to her father's strategy for

[13] Strachey, *Historie*, Cap. VIII, 102.

[14] The conversation between Pocahontas and Smith in London in 1616 furnishes evidence that she was present when Smith and Powhatan held their parley at Werowocomoco in 1609. Though seven years had elapsed, Pocahontas could quote verbatim certain things that had been said at the parley. Smith, *Generall Historie*, Book IV, 122.

dealing with the Jamestown colonists. It was obviously a strategy born of frustration. Seated on his bed-throne with Pocahontas by his side, and surrounded by wives, children, other relatives, and warriors, Powhatan bluntly asked Smith what he was doing in Werowocomoco, denying that he had extended an invitation or made any promise of corn. If Smith wanted corn, he would have to pay for it—one sword or gun for every bushel. Smith chided Powhatan for his "forgetfullness," pointing out to him the very warriors who had come to Jamestown bearing Powhatan's invitation, at which Chief Powhatan gave out with "a merry laughter."[15]

Then Powhatan agreed to look at the commodities the colonists wished to trade for corn, though he repeated firmly that "none he liked without gunnes and Swords."[16] Smith, growing irritated, reminded Powhatan that the colonists were neglecting the work of their "glass factory" at Jamestown by sending laborers to build Powhatan's house. Yet the colonists were being denied provisions because Powhatan had told the tribes living near Jamestown not to trade with the colonists. "As for swords and gunnes," Smith said, "I told you long agoe I had none to spare; and you must know those I have can keepe me from want; yet stele or wrong you I will not, nor dissolve that friendship we have mutually promised, except you constrain me by your bad usage."[17]

Powhatan listened attentively to Smith's words. Then he made his standard play: "Some doubt I have of your coming hither, that makes me not so kindly seeke to relieve you as I would: for many doe informe me, your coming hither is not for trade but to invade my people, and possess my Country, who dare not come to bring you Corne, seeing you thus armed with your men. To

[15] *Ibid.*, 75.
[16] *Ibid.*
[17] *Ibid.*

free us of this feare, leave abbord your weapons, for here they are needless."[18] It was clear that to disarm the English was still Powhatan's one desire.

Powhatan and Smith continued their verbal exchange, matching wits to determine who was going to govern the other. Both men employed flattery and threats. Lay down your arms, Powhatan said, "we being all friends and forever Powhatans."[19] Smith said that he would not yield an inch on that matter. The Powhatan warriors were never asked to discard their bows and arrows when they came to Jamestown. Besides, Smith loftily announced, trying to bluff the chief, the Powhatan's "friendly care"[20] was needless, for the colonists had other ways of procuring food that Powhatan did not know about. Then Powhatan, with sorrowful countenance, ordered his people to bring some corn from the royal storehouse but qualified the order: "Captain Smith, I never used any werowance so kindly as yourselfe, yet from you I receive the least kindness of any . . . if you intend so friendly as you say, send hence your armes that I may beleeve you."[21] Smith again refused. Powhatan's people carried the corn from the storehouse but made no effort to load it onto the barges, and Smith had to summon the crewmen to shore to see to the loading themselves.

Powhatan, realizing that the battle of wits was getting him nowhere, arose and departed, to continue his machinations from afar. He left some warriors milling about outside his palace, and Smith and John Russell, still inside and fearing they were in danger, rushed out and drove the warriors away. Then they returned to their quarters near shore. That evening Powhatan sent Smith "a great bracelet and chaine of pearle" with the mes-

[18] *Ibid.*
[19] *Ibid.*
[20] *Ibid.*, 76.
[21] *Ibid.*

sage that he had left the conference because he was afraid of the guns, and "knowing when the ice was broken there would come more men, sent these numbers but to guard his corn from stealing, that might happen without your knowledge: now though some bee hurt by your misprision [bad behavior], yet Powhatan is your friend, and so will forever continue."[22] Then Powhatan gave Smith permission to send the corn back to Jamestown but said that if he himself wished to stay at Werowocomoco he would have to put away his arms. Once again Smith refused to do so.

The next day Smith supervised the loading of the barges, but the task was not finished by nightfall, and the colonists were compelled to spend another night among the Powhatans. Since their provisions were exhausted, Smith sent word to Chief Powhatan asking for food. While the colonists were waiting for a reply, Pocahontas arrived at their quarters. She came, as William Phettiplace, Anas Todkill, Jeffry Abbot, and Richard Wiffin later testified, to save their lives.

When she arrived, having come "that darke night . . . through the irksome woods," she warned Smith that the chief would send them food but that "Powhatan and all the power he could make, would after[ward] come kill us all, if they that brought it could not kill us with our owne weapons when we were at supper."[23]

Smith now realized, if indeed he had not done so earlier, that Powhatan's protestations of friendship and concern were merely deceptive rhetoric and that the concessions he had made to the colonists—the food he had given them, the hospitality he had provided—were part of a strategy leading not to any ultimate reconciliation between Indian and colonist but, at the advantageous moment, to the extermination of the English.

Smith was deeply grateful for Pocahontas' warning and for

[22] *Ibid.*, 77.
[23] *Ibid.*

her intervention in the contest she had tried on so many earlier occasions to bring to an end. He tried to thank her, and "such things as shee would have delighted in, he would have given her: but with the teares running downe her cheekes she said she durst not be seene to have any: for if Powhatan should know it, she were but dead."[24] And so, having once again played her part in the Jamestown drama, "shee ranne away by herselfe as she came."[25]

Shortly thereafter, eight or ten stalwart Powhatans arrived, bringing food. Smith insisted that the Powhatans taste each dish of food before he and his companions ate from it. Then he sent the Indians back to their chief with a message that if the chief had anything further to add to their earlier conversation he must come to the colonists' hut immediately, for Smith was preparing to leave. Powhatan, probably sensing that Smith was prepared to do battle, did not come to the hut or send warriors in his stead. Smith departed the next day. The two men never met again.

Soon after Smith and his companions left Werowocomoco, Pocahontas saved the life of still another Englishman, colonist Richard Wiffin. Wiffin had set out from Jamestown alone to report to Smith the grim news of the deaths of Captain Scrivener, Richard Waldo, Anthony Gosnold, and eight other colonists.[26] Scrivener, temporary president of the colony, had ignored express instructions to remain in Jamestown until Smith's return, and had delegated Captain Peter Winne to act as commandant of the fort while he took a party of colonists to the Isle of Hogs in the James River to shoot fowl, wild hogs, and other game. The skiff in which they sailed had sunk, and all members of the party had drowned.[27]

24 *Ibid.*
25 *Ibid.*
26 *Ibid.*, 86.
27 *Ibid.*, 73.

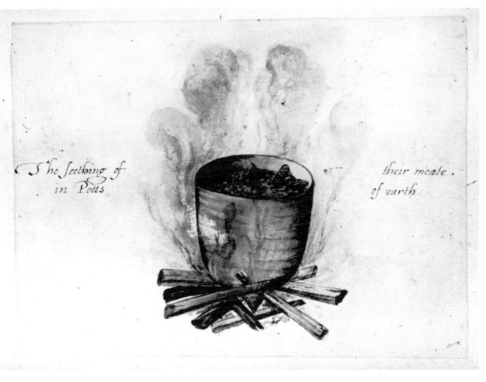

Cooking in a pot. Water color by John White, 1585.

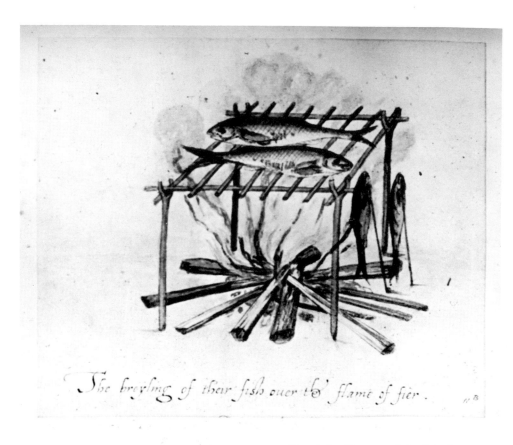

The broyling of their fish ouer the flame of fier.

Cooking fish. Water color by John White, 1585.

102

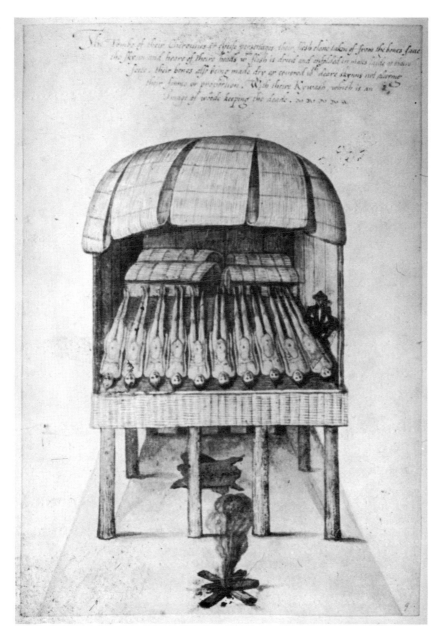

Indian charnal house. Water color by John White, 1585.

The "Lyte Jewel," seventeenth-century gold pendant, enameled and set with diamonds, containing a miniature portrait of King James I. In the British Museum, London.

Captain George Percy, twice governor of Jamestown and younger brother of the ninth Earl of Northumberland. Original in Syon House, Brentford, England.

Courtesy Thomas Gilcrease Institute of History and Art, Tulsa

Thomas West, Third Lord de la Warr. From the original portrait by Wybrandt De Geest.

Sir Thomas Dale, governor of Virginia.

Eustace Rolfe, grandfather of John Rolfe.

En route to Werowocomoco with news of the disaster, Wiffin "was encountered with many dangers and difficulties in all parts as he passed" surreptitiously among the Powhatans, who kept watch for "such straungers as should invade their territories."[28] By the time Wiffin reached Werowocomoco, he was half-frozen and ill from hunger, and all he could perceive in the Powhatan capital were "preparations for warre." There was no sign of Captain Smith.[29]

Fortunately for Wiffin, Pocahontas discovered his presence at just about the same time the Powhatan warriors did. Realizing that "some mischiefe was intended" toward him, she "hid him for a time, and sent them who pursued him the cleane contrary way to seek him," saving him from capture and probable death "by her meanes and extraordinary bribes, and much trouble."[30]

Then Pocahontas told Wiffin how to reach Smith, who was on his way to Menapucunt, Opechancanough's village, in search of more provisions. Wiffin reached Menapucunt without mishap. There he found Smith and his men in the midst of "turmoyles."[31] On their arrival they had observed that Opechancanough's warriors outnumbered them by hundreds. Certain that the formidable chief would imitate Powhatan's increasingly overt treachery, Smith, John Russell, and George Percy had rushed into his lodge, where Smith, in his own words, "did take this murdering Opechancanough . . . by the long locke on his head, and with my pistole at his breast, I led him before his greatest forces, and before we parted made him fill our Bark of twenty tuns of corne."[32] It was while Smith, gun in hand, was supervising the loading of the corn and "200 weight of venison and suet" that Wiffin arrived with his news. Smith quickly brought his dealings

[28] Strachey, *Historie*, Cap. VIII, 101–102.
[29] Smith, *Generall Historie*, Book III, 80.
[30] *Ibid.*
[31] *Ibid.*
[32] Smith, *New England Trials*, C2.

with Opechancanough to an end and hastened back to Jamestown.

Smith was to make no more food-gathering expeditions among the Powhatans. For the remainder of the time he served as the administrator of Jamestown, he was to concentrate upon making the colony as nearly self-sufficient as possible. From his last expedition among the Powhatans he had reached two conclusions. First, the colonists could "dreame no longer of this vain hope from Powhatan"[33] of peaceful and constructive co-operation. Second, without the support of their one real friend among the Powhatans, the young Pocahontas, he and many other Englishmen would have been killed, and the Jamestown colony would have been doomed.

[33] Smith, *Generall Historie, Book* III, 86.

CHAPTER IX

The Starving Time

As JAMESTOWN ENTERED ITS THIRD YEAR of existence, Smith inaugurated a new work program to strengthen the colony, hoping to make it invulnerable to the growing militancy of the Powhatans. Chief Powhatan was making ever bolder moves against the colonists. While Smith was taking the long water route home, Powhatan persuaded the colonists who were building his house to return to Jamestown overland to obtain swords, pikes, muskets, and hatchets on the pretext that Smith had requisitioned them. Captain Peter Winne, who was in charge of supplies at

Jamestown, believed the request legitimate and had sent back the weapons and tools, inadvertently contributing to Powhatan's arsenal.

Anxious for the future, Smith decided to enlarge the fort and to dig a deep well that would supply enough water to serve an even larger number of colonists than were presently at Jamestown. He also ordered laborers to clear, plow, and plant thirty acres of ground on the high ridges of the island. Tassore and Kemps, two Powhatan prisoners, were pressed into service to teach the colonists the Indian way of planting beans, corn, and pumpkins.

English gentlemen who had never done a day's labor in their lives were ordered to fell trees and split logs,[1] and Smith supervised the building of a blockhouse on the neck of land at the north end of Jamestown Peninsula, hoping thus to prevent the Chickahominies from entering Jamestown by its back door and stealing the colonists' supplies. The men stationed at the blockhouse were "to entertaine the Salvages trade . . . [but permit] none to passe nor repasse Salvage nor Christian Without the President's order."[2] In the spring of 1609, trying to prove to the Powhatans that the colonists could indeed supply their own needs, Smith sent "60 or 80 [colonists] with Ensign Laxon . . . down the river to live upon Oysters, and 20 with lieutenant Percy to try for fishing at Poynt Comfort, Master West with as many went up the falls, but nothing could be found there but acorns."[3]

Smith's strengthening of the colony was his last official service for Jamestown. In July, 1609, Captain Samuel Argall arrived from England and gave Smith the news that on May 23, 1609, a second charter had been granted to the Virginia Company of

[1] When the axes the gentlemen wielded blistered their hands, they sometimes "blasphemed their creator." As punishment Smith ordered his soldiers to dash a dipper of cold water down their sleeves.
[2] Smith, *Generall Historie*, Book III, 86.
[3] *Ibid.*

London, unyoking it from the North Virginia Company and abolishing the Jamestown council. The new company, the Treasurer and Company of Adventurers and Planters of the City of London for the First Colony in Virginia,[4] would govern Jamestown through its Supreme Council, sitting in London, and direct rule of the colony would be vested in a governor, with lifetime tenure of office. Lord De La Warr had been appointed to the office but had not yet left England for Jamestown. Argall reported, moreover, that nine ships had been scheduled to sail from England on June 1 as a demonstration of the new company's optimistic plans for revitalizing Jamestown.

Smith did not wait for the arrival of the new governor but immediately relinquished the presidency to George Percy and made plans to build himself a home away from Jamestown, near the falls at Parahunt's village. Smith had always been extraordinarily independent and had seldom been able to work successfully under another's command. When he learned of the return to the colony of Gabriel Archer and John Ratcliffe, with whom he had quarreled and who had returned to London and charged him with mismanaging the colony and leading it to failure,[5] Smith simply decided to set himself apart and live on his own terms. He went to the falls and obtained some land from Parahunt, but while returning by boat to Jamestown to arrange for the construction of a house (which he planned to call "Nonesuch"), a bag of gunpowder he was carrying exploded, burning him severely. His injuries were slow to heal, and finally he was compelled to return to England for medical treatment. He set sail on October 1, 1609, probably on board the *Falcon*, one of

[4] Virtually independent of either Parliament or king, the newly organized company was sponsored by Sir Francis Bacon and Robert Cecil, Earl of Salisbury, together with 21 peers, 96 knights, 10 clergymen and physicians, 53 officers, 28 members of the gentry, and 110 merchants. (Brown, *The Genesis of the United States*, I, 206–30; Neill, *History of the Virginia Company*, 32.)

[5] Smith, *Travels and Works of Captain John Smith*, I, 168–69.

seven ships that had recently brought hundreds of new colonists to Virginia.[6]

Smith's departure marked the beginning of the colony's most grievous days, though none in Jamestown realized it at the time. His absence and that of Pocahontas meant that the colony was deprived of the two people who had most earnestly struggled for accommodation between the English and the Powhatans. Though Smith had been aggressive and militant, he had earned the Indians' respect, if not their love, and certainly his friendly association with Pocahontas had for a time helped lessen the tensions between the colonists and the natives. Smith was never to return to Virginia, and three long years were to pass before Pocahontas would be seen in Jamestown again.

Without the peace-keeping influence of Smith and Pocahontas the latent hostility of the Indians flared into overt acts of destruction. Richard Potts and William Tankard, the new recorders of the colony, attested that "the salvages no sooner understood Smith was gone but they all revolted and did spoile and murther all they encountered."[7]

Powhatan's War had begun. According to George Percy, Indians in war paint made ferocious attacks on the colony. Howling Weanocs, Chickahominies, and Chiskiacks preyed on the colonists and made their lives miserable. The Indians sang a new song, composed, it was said, by Parahunt's people, the message of the song being that the savages now killed the colonists not because they were a foreign people but "for all their poccasacks [guns]" and for their other weapons, their hatchets, poleaxes, and English pikes. Indeed, it was a war for the acquisition of power and weaponry.

[6] Smith's arrival in England in December, 1609, made King James exceedingly happy. In accordance with instructions from Robert Cecil, the Lord Treasurer, Smith had brought along a pair of flying squirrels which the king very much wanted.

[7] Smith, *Generall Historie*, Book IV, 105.

With the opening of hostilities the Powhatans boasted that "for all that Captain Newport had brought them copper, they could kill 'Symon,' a youthful prisoner."[8] To assure their victory, they held the elaborate ritualistic sacrifice of youths of the tribe.

Chief Powhatan directed the war from his new seat of government at Rasawrack. There he conceived a plot to kill a number of the colonists in one blow. The plot involved young Thomas Savage, the English boy who had been left with Powhatan to learn the Indians' language and culture. Savage had become a favorite of Powhatan's; the chief called him "my boy," employed him as an interpreter, and permitted him to eat from his own royal platter.

In the autumn of 1609, Powhatan sent Savage to Jamestown accompanied by several Indians carrying provisions for the colony—wild turkeys, venison, and baskets heaped high with maize. Savage presented the gifts to Percy, the temporary council president, who interpreted them as a hopeful sign that Powhatan's War might soon end. Certainly Percy, not yet thirty years old, in ill-health himself and watching helplessly as his fellow colonists died of plague and yellow fever, yearned for peace with the Indians. He accepted Powhatan's provisions with gratitude and arranged for some blue glass beads and woolen fabrics to be sent to the chief in return.

Young Savage did not return to Rasawrack with the Indians. Though he had seemed satisfied among the Indians, now he was reluctant to return to them unless accompanied by one of his own countrymen.[9] Percy agreed to send young Henry Spelman with him—much to Spelman's annoyance. Spelman, the scapegoat son of an English aristocrat, had arrived only recently in Jamestown. Soon after his arrival he had accompanied Smith on his journey to Parahunt's village to arrange for the land for his

[8] Strachey, "The First Booke," Cap. 5, 34.
[9] Brown, "Spelman's Relation," *The Genesis of the United States*, I, 483–88.

115

new home. Smith had left Spelman at the falls with Parahunt when he went back to Jamestown,[10] expecting, of course, to return. After waiting in vain, Spelman had had to make his way back to Jamestown on his own. He had no desire to become another Thomas Savage, living among the natives and learning their languages and ways.

Nevertheless, Spelman accompanied Thomas Savage to Rasawrack, and found the Indian capital not too unpleasant. Warmly welcomed by Powhatan, Spelman was accorded the same honors as those bestowed on Savage. He was permitted to eat with the chief, and was waited upon by Powhatan's slaves. The two boys roamed Rasawrack at will, wandering as far as Uttamussack, on the Pamunkey River,[11] and even entering one of Powhatan's house temples, where Spelman saw the English bed, the copper crown, and the basin and ewer that King James had sent from England the year before.[12]

After remaining about three weeks at Rasawrack, Spelman returned to Jamestown, carrying a message from Powhatan to Captain Percy and other members of the council: If the colonists would "bring ther ship and sum copper he [Powhatan] would fraught [freight] her backe with corn."[13] Percy, hopeful that Powhatan might be genuinely interested in a peaceful relationship with the colonists, sent Spelman back to inform the chief that he would send the ship to Werowocomoco, where the royal storehouses were still located.

Without delay sixty-two colonists in two boats, one manned by Captain Ratcliffe and the other by William West, the nephew of Lord De La Warr, started up the Pamunkey River. Reaching

[10] *Ibid.*, 484.

[11] McCary, *Indians in Seventeenth-Century Virginia*, 57. McCary's identification of early Powhatan sites in Tidewater Virginia has been of great value to historians and archaeologists.

[12] Brown, "Spelman's Relation," *The Genesis of the United States*, I, 483–88.

[13] *Ibid.*, 484–85.

Werowocomoco, they went ashore, "Captain West and Captain Sicklemore [Ratcliffe] each with a small ship and each with thirtie or fortie men well appointed sought abroad to trade."[14]

But the colonists were to find not trade but ambush and death. "Sicklemore . . . with about thirtie others as careless as himself were all slaine; only Jeffry Shortridge escaped."[15] Sixty colonists were massacred by the Powhatans. A boy named Samuel was taken prisoner. Shortridge brought back the tragic news to Jamestown.

The massacre was a devastating blow to Jamestown. It seemed almost impossible to continue after such a loss, which robbed the colonists of much of their will to survive. Without corn there was no sustenance, and with the Powhatans' hostility now so intense there was little reason to seek help from the natives. Never since the founding of Jamestown had the colony been in such desperate straits. That bleak winter of 1609–10 was ever afterward to be known as the "starving time." In six months the population dropped from 490 to 60. In their last extremities the colonists revealed their agonies in tragic and erratic ways. One colonist killed his wife and was found eating her salted remains.[16] His trial and execution did not deter other colonists from roasting and eating an Indian killed during an attack on the fort.

So appalling did the situation become, while Powhatan waged war against them and they huddled in the final stages of starvation, that one Jamestown colonist, in utter despair, cast his Bible into the communal fire, crying out, "Alas, there is no God!"[17]

[14] *Ibid.*; see also Smith, *Travels and Works of Captain John Smith*, I, 498.

[15] Brown, "Spelman's Relation," *The Genesis of the United States*, I, 484–85.

[16] Neill, *History of the Virginia Company*, 32; Purchas, *Purchas His Pilgrimes*, IV, 1759.

[17] Brown, *The Genesis of the United States*, II, 996; Fiske, *Old Virginia and Her Neighbors*, I, 182; Purchas, *Purchas His Pilgrimes*, IV, 1757; Neill, *History of the Virginia Company*, 32.

CHAPTER X

A Second Chance

JAMESTOWN WAS DYING. England's great hopes for colonizing in the New World seemed to be coming to nought. Sir Walter Raleigh's enthusiastic claim of 1602, "I shall yet live to see in Virginia an English Nation,"[1] rang hollow, and the optimism of the backers of the effort appeared unlikely to save the distant settlement. In 1609 the Lord Mayor of London was urging the great livery companies of London to buy shares in the new Virginia Company, to rid the city of "a swarm of unhappy persons

[1] Alexander Wilbourne Weddell (ed.), *Virginia Historical Portraiture*, 70.

who infested their streets, the cause of plague and famine, and entice them to Virginia,"[2] and such publications as *Nova Britannia, Good Speed to Virginia,* and *Virginia Richly Valued*[3] were encouraging Englishmen to seek their fortunes in the New World.[4] Meanwhile, the Jamestown colony was suffering what seemed to be its final death agonies.

Yet Jamestown had never been more important to England. Her old enemy Spain had been deeply concerned about the attempt at colonization and had kept close watch on her successes and failures in the New World. Pedro de Zúñiga, the Spanish ambassador to the Court of St. James's, sent frequent reports in code to his ruler, Philip III, to which Philip would respond, as he did on May 14, 1609: "All that you say touching Virginia is well understood here and attention is paid to what may be proper to do in this matter."[5] Philip was indeed interested in knowing whether Protestant England was going to succeed in the New World. Whenever he learned of ships leaving for Virginia, he asked for details: "Concerning what you say of the progress made there in fortifying Virginia, and the number of people whom they wish to send there, you must be on the look out, to report when those will depart who are to settle that country, with what forces they go, and what route they will have to take in their voyage hither—so that here, such orders may be given as will be necessary."[6]

2 Neill, *History of the Virginia Company,* 25.

3 *Ibid.,* 25–26.

4 Obviously weary of reading the many tracts designed to encourage emigration to Virginia, the Most Reverend Tobias Matthew, Archbishop of York, petulantly wrote to the Earl of Somerset (then a favorite of King James's): "Of Virginia there are so many tractates divine, human, historical, political, or call them as you please, as no further intelligence I dare desire." Neill, *History of the Virginia Company,* 26.

5 Brown, *The Genesis of the United States,* I, 311.

6 *Ibid.*

Thus, in 1610, Philip was delighted to hear from his new ambassador to England, Alonso de Velasco, that the Jamestown attempt seemed to have ended in total failure, a failure that perhaps prepared the way for Spanish acquisition of the Virginia territory:

> The Indians hold the English surrounded in the strong place which they had erected there, having killed the larger part of them, and the others were left, so entirely without provisions, that, they thought it impossible to escape, because the survivors eat the dead, and when one of the natives died fighting, they dug him up again, two days afterwards to be eaten. The swine which they carried there . . . the Indians killed and almost all who came . . . died from having eaten dogs, Cat skins and other vile stuff. Unless they succour them with some provisions in an English ship . . . they must have perished before this. Thus it looks as if the zeal for this enterprise was cooling off and it would . . . on this account be very easy to make an end of it altogether by sending out a few ships to finish what might be left in that place.[7]

But while Philip was contemplating the invasion of Virginia, other events were occurring that were to give Jamestown a new lease on life. English luck and English determination combined to save the colony.

On May 23, 1610, the colonists who had survived the horrors of the previous winter saw two ships drop anchor off the Jamestown Peninsula. The ships were English, and they were appropriately named: the *Deliverance* and the *Patience*. The arrival of the ships marked the end of a six-month nightmare.

The *Deliverance* and the *Patience* had come to Jamestown only by the most difficult route and under the most unlikely circumstances. Almost a year before, on June 1, 1609, the *Sea Ven-*

[7] *Ibid.*, 392.

ture, flagship of the Virginia Company's nine-ship fleet, set sail from England bound for Virginia. Flying both the Union Jack and the flag of Scotland, the *Sea Venture* carried such distinguished passengers as Sir Thomas Gates, the newly elected deputy governor of the Virginia colony; Sir George Somers, the commander of the fleet; Christopher Newport, who was making one more trip across the Atlantic; William Strachey, a member of the Children of the Queens Revels, the London acting company, and a friend of Shakespeare's; the Reverend Richard Bucke, who was to succeed Mr. Hunt; and the Indian boy, Namontack, returning with another Powhatan boy, Matchumps, from a visit to England. The *Sea Venture* carried about one hundred prospective colonists, as well as "all manner of directions and provisions." Sailing west for the New World, the *Sea Venture* encountered a hurricane, became separated from the fleet, and was presumed lost.[8] Actually the ship managed to reach Bermuda, where it foundered and was wrecked. The survivors spent nine or ten months building two pinnaces, the *Deliverance* and the *Patience*, from timber they salvaged from the flagship. William Strachey kept a record of the survivors' adventures in Bermuda, noting that during the time it took to build the ships Elizabeth Persons, Mistress Horton's maidservant, married Thomas Powell, Sir George Somer's cook; two children were born and christened; and two murders were committed, one by Robert Waters, a sailor, who killed a companion with a shovel,

---

[8] The Spanish ambassador, Zúñiga, reported the loss of the *Sea Venture* to King Philip in a letter dated December 19, 1609: "I have received a letter in which I am told that three vessles of those which sailed down here to Virginia have returned to the Downs. They confirm what I have written Y.M. that the Captain's ship was lost with the most distinguished people who went, and the *Orders* according to which they were to be governed in that part. . . . I shall continue to give an account of all I may hear to Y.M. whose Catholic Person Our Lord preserve as all Christendom needeth." (Brown, *The Genesis of the United States*, I, 336–37.)

and the other by Matchumps, who in a fit of anger killed Namontack.[9]

When the two pinnaces were completed, the survivors, somewhat depleted in numbers, sailed away from Bermuda, making their way to their original Virginia destination. Sir Thomas Gates had managed to save the administrative orders and instructions for the colony and planned to assume office and guide Jamestown toward the pre-eminence that the Virginia Company so eagerly envisioned for it.

Upon their arrival at Jamestown, Gates and his party were met by desperate colonists, many of them dying, others wandering desolately about the ruins of the settlement. Gates realized that his first duty was to save the people, even if it meant abandoning the colony. He inspected the settlement and reported:

> Viewing the Fort, we found the Pallisadoes torne downe, the Ports open, the Gates from off the hinges, and emptie houses (which Owners' death had taken from them) rent up and burnt rather than the dwellers would step into the woods a stones castoff from them, to fetch other fire-wood: and it is true, the Indians killed without, if our men stirred beyond the bounds of their Block-house, as [many as] Famine and Pestilence did within. . . . In this desolation misery our Governour found the condition and state of our Colonie.[10]

Gates conferred with Percy and the other survivors, hoping to find some way to preserve the colony, but he soon agreed with them that little could be done in the face of Powhatan's crushing hostility:

> The Indians . . . were forbidden likewise (by their subtile King at all to trade with us); and not only so, but to endanger and assault any Boate upon the River, or stragler out of the Fort by Land, by

[9] Purchas, *Purchas His Pilgrimes*, IV, 1746.
[10] *Ibid.*, 1749.

which (not long before our arrival) our people had a large Boate cut off, and divers of our men killed, even within command of our Block-house; as likewise, they shot two of our people to death, after we had bin foure and five dayes come in . . . .[11]

Gates, Somers, and Newport were seasoned veterans of wars in the Netherlands and in Ireland and were well qualified to assess the military aspects of the situation. Grimly, they decided to abandon Jamestown. The colony's survivors would be placed aboard the *Deliverance* and the *Patience* and, together with the survivors of the wreck of the *Sea Venture*, would return to England.

On June 7, 1610, Gates ordered his men to strip the huts of possessions and load them on the ships. To the accompaniment of funereal drum rolls, the colonists boarded the ships, sixty survivors of the nine hundred men, women, and children who had come to Jamestown since 1607. The ships weighed anchor and started down the James River toward the sea. At nightfall the ships' crews dropped anchor at Mulberry Island, planning to head into the Atlantic at daybreak.

So it was that the colonists were saved, though Jamestown itself seemed a dead cause. The nightmare on the peninsula had ended but with it all England's hopes for colonial expansion in the New World. Or so it seemed.

In the early-morning light of June 8, 1610, while still at anchor at Mulberry Island, the *Patience* and *Deliverance* passengers saw three ships silhouetted on the horizon, heading upstream toward them. Within a few hours they had made contact with the ships, and with Lord De La Warr, the governor of the Virginia Company, who had decided to come to the New World to see for himself how matters stood in Jamestown. It was an almost miraculously opportune meeting. Had De La Warr ar-

11 *Ibid.*, 1750.

rived only hours later, he would not have found a single Englishman to govern. As it was, he turned the ships around and
recommenced the Jamestown experiment, instilling in the colonists once again the spirit of commitment that destitution had
wrung from them.

De La Warr had been appointed supreme governor of the
colony in 1609, and on February 21 of that year had listened
to the admonishment of the Reverend William Crashaw, who
preached at the Temple in honor of the appointment:

> And thou most noble Lord, whom God hath stirred up to neglect
> the pleasures of England, and with Abraham to go from thy coun-
> try, and forsake thy kindred and thy father's house, to go to a land
> which God will show thee, give me leave to speak the truth. Thy
> ancestor many hundred years ago gained great honour to thy house
> but by this action thou augmenst it. . . . Remember, thou art a
> general of English men, nay a general of Christian men; therefore
> principally look to religion. You go to commend it to the Heathen,
> then practice it yourselves; make the name of Christ honourable,
> not hateful unto them.[12]

So inspired, and after ample preparation and long study, De La
Warr finally sailed for the New World in April, 1610, with a fleet
of three ships carrying 150 new colonists. The flagship, the *De
La Warr*, carried the governor himself and fifty scarlet-liveried
attendants.

After meeting the refugees, he ordered Sir Thomas Gates to
conduct everyone back to Jamestown. Stepping foot onto the
peninsula on June 10, De La Warr reportedly fell to his knees
and thanked God that he had come in time to save Jamestown.
He had to admit, however, that it was "a verie noysome and
unholsome place,"[13] and he was deeply disturbed by the sight
that presented itself at the abandoned colony.

[12] Neill, *History of the Virginia Company*, 35.

Entering the fort through the south gate with standards flying, De La Warr went immediately to the church, where amid the ruins Mr. Bucke delivered a sermon. Then De La Warr's commission was read, whereupon Gates relinquished to him the administration of the colony, and De La Warr made a speech of acceptance.[14] Next he summoned Gates, Percy, and others to a conference to assemble information about Jamestown for a report to be sent to the Supreme Council in England, along with his own plans for rehabilitating the colony.

In the report he observed that much of the misery he saw at Jamestown had, in part, been

> occasioned bie the mortalitie and Idleness of our owne people, whereupon the next Daie I sett the sailors to worke to unloade shippes and the landmen some to cleanse the towne, some to make cole for the forges. I sent fisherman out to provide fish for our men, to save other provision, but these had but ill success. Likewise I Dispached Sir George Sommers back Againe to the Barmudas . . . and if it please God, he doe Saflie return, he will store us with hoges . . . fleshe, and fishe enoughe to serve the whole colonie this wynter. Thus bie God's assistance I shall goe forwards Imploying my best indevors in settlinge and managing these affaires.[15]

De La Warr set working hours from six to ten in the morning and from two to four in the afternoon. The church bell summoned colonists to their respective tasks, as well as to the church itself for twice-daily services, as attested to by Strachey, now the recorder of the colony:

> First they enter into the Church and make their praiers unto God, next they returne to their houses and receive their proportion of

[13] Brown, *The Genesis of the United States*, I, 415.
[14] Smith, *Generall Historie*, Book IV, 106.
[15] *Ibid.*

food. Nor should it be conceived that this business excluded Gentlemen whose breeding never knew what a daies labour meant, for
though they cannot dig, use the Spade, nor practice the Axe finde
how to employ [their] knowledge.[16]

The church building was rebuilt and refurbished. It was now
sixty feet long and twenty-four feet wide, with a cedar chancel,
a black-walnut communion table, and cedar pews. There were
"faire broad windowes to shut and open," as well as a pulpit, a
font, and two bells at the west end.[17] On orders from De La
Warr, there were wildflowers in the church at all times. Sunday
services were elaborate. Mr. Bucke preached two sermons, and
De La Warr and his officers dressed for the occasion, wearing
slashed velvet, ruffs, and jeweled accessories. De Le Warr's chair
was elegantly draped with green velvet, and at his feet was a
scarlet kneeling cushion. Following the services the governor
entertained on board the *De La Warr*, where he lived throughout his nine-month stay at Jamestown.

De La Warr left for England on March 28, 1611. De La Warr
apprised Robert Cecil, the Earl of Salisbury (James's minister
of the treasury) in June that "he is weak from sickness, but would
not have returned so suddenly if the winds had [not] favoured
his voyage for the West Indies, at his departure from Virginia.
That country is in a most hopeful state."[18] His leadership had
by no means solved all the problems of the colony. There were
still problems of recurring food shortage, illness, accidental
death, and Indian attacks. Somers had died on the way to Bermuda for provisions. De La Warr himself had suffered from gout,
dysentery, and scurvy, though he had been well treated by Dr.
Laurence Bohun, his private physician. None of the new leaders,

[16] *Ibid.*, 107.

[17] Fiske, *Old Virginia and Her Neighbors*, I, 160–61.

[18] Vol. LXIV, 518 State Papers Domestic James I, Public Record Office,
London.

De La Warr or his assistants, had made significant progress in ending Powhatan's War.

Yet De La Warr's leadership had given Jamestown a second chance. He had restored order and stability to the colony, clarified its significance for its members, and once again formalized its institutions. Moreover, he had encouraged private enterprise, which had been provided for in the second charter. Each colonist had been given his own plot of ground to cultivate, and communal farming had been abolished. This improvement in the economic functioning of the colony raised morale at Jamestown and brought forth renewed effort by the members. When De La Warr left, Jamestown had new courage to face the future. Once again Captain Percy assumed temporary command of the colony, awaiting the arrival of the High Marshal of Virginia, Sir Thomas Dale, who was to arrive in May, 1611, and serve until Sir Thomas Gates, who had returned to England in September, 1610, arrived in Virginia again.

CHAPTER XI

Signs of Success

POCAHONTAS COULD NOT come to Jamestown Peninsula to examine the revived colony. Open contact with the English was prevented by the dictates of her father and by the war her people continued to wage against the English. Yet she did not willingly accept the limitations upon her activities and did not altogether acquiesce in her father's commands. Ever since the massacre of the sixty colonists in 1609, she had been at odds with her father's policies, and, as John Smith was to observe many years later,

128

there was strife between her and Chief Powhatan during the "long and troublesome warre after my departure."[1]

Pocahontas spent an increasing amount of time away from Rasawrack, her father's new capital. Early in 1610, shortly after the massacre, she settled among the less militant and hostile Patawomekes (Potomacs), ostensibly as a tax collector for her father but also as a refugee from the conflict. The Patawomekes' principal villages were about ninety miles north of Rasawrack on a pleasant bluff overlooking an arm of Potomac Creek and the Potomac River beyond. The tribe, which numbered about 750 people, was one of the larger tribes in the Powhatan Confederacy—and one of the richest. The principal chief was Pasptanze.[2]

While among the Patawomekes, far removed from the affairs of Jamestown, Pocahontas had an opportunity to help at least one Englishman, young Henry Spelman, who had been stranded among the Powhatans after the massacre. Having inadvertently played a role in the massacre by acting as messenger of Powhatan, Spelman was eager to escape from the household of the chief. Soon after Pocahontas went to live among the Patawomekes, she and Pasptanze journeyed to Rasawrack, probably to deliver tax collections to the Powhatan storehouses, and there they learned that Spelman wanted to leave Rasawrack, as did young Thomas Savage and the boy named Samuel, who had been taken prisoner during the attack.

As Spelman was later to tell it, "The King of Patomeck came to visit the great Powhatan, when being awhile with him, he shewed such kindness to Savage, Samuell, and myself, as we determined to goe away with him."[3] On the day Pocahontas and

---

[1] Smith, *Generall Historie*, Book IV, 105.

[2] Thomas De La Warr, *The Relation of the Right Honourable the Lord De La Warre, Lord Governour and Captaine Generall of the Colonie Planted in Virginia*; hereafter cited as *Relation*. See also Brown, *The Genesis of the United States*, I, 483.

[3] Brown, *The Genesis of the United States*, I, 487.

Pasptanze set out on the return journey to Patawomeke, the three boys stole away with them. As chance and human nature would have it, however, the boys' escape was not to be so easy. "Having gone a mile or too on the way Savage fayned some excuse to stay and unbeknownst to us went back to the Powhatan and acquainted him with our departing with ye Patawomeke (Potomac)."[4] Young Savage, Powhatan's pet, had been with the Indians too long; he had transferred his loyalty to the chief. As a result, "The Powhatan presently sends after us commanding our returne, which we refusing, went still on our way: and those that weare sent went still on with us, till one of them . . . suddenly strooke Samuell with an axe and killed him, which I seenge ran away."[5]

Pocahontas and Pasptanze were unable to defend the boys from Powhatan's warriors, but after Spelman made his escape, they were able to provide sanctuary and care for him. According to Captain Argall, who later heard the story from Spelman himself, "Pokahontas the King's daughter saved a boy called Henry Spelman that lived many years afterwards by her meanes among the Patawomekes."[6] Spelman thus acknowledged that it was Pocahontas who was primarily responsible for his survival and for his friendly acceptance among the Patawomekes, with whom he stayed until he could rejoin his own countrymen.

The most significant aspect of Pocahontas' assistance to Spelman was that it gave the English an opportunity to report to London that there were some hopeful signs in English-Indian

[4] *Ibid.*

[5] *Ibid.*

[6] Smith, *Travels and Works of Captain John Smith*, II, 498. It is unlikely that a stranger would have been able to find the Patawomekes' villages without help from the Indians. The region was not frequented by explorers; ossuaries of the Potomacs found by T. Dale Stewart, who excavated the site, yielded very few white men's trade goods. (See T. Dale Stewart, "Excavating the Indian Village of Patawomeke," *Explorations and Field Work of the Smithsonian Institution in 1938*, 87–90.)

relations. Such a report would help persuade more Englishmen to venture across the Atlantic and to swell the numbers of colonists to a size large enough to overwhelm the Powhatans. Certainly one of the reasons for the colonists' difficulties in the early years was their small numbers. And as reports of their sufferings and hardships circulated in England, enthusiasm for colonization waned. Everyone concerned with colonizing the New World realized the advantage of favorable reports from Virginia.

Lord De La Warr had revitalized Jamestown and had given new life to the colonial experiment. But now there was need to make colonial life attractive. In September, 1610, during De La Warr's stay in Jamestown, Captain Argall sailed for Bermuda, became lost, and found himself on the Potomac River. He chanced upon a friendly village of Patawomekes with young Spelman safe and sound in their midst and Pocahontas, the friendliest of all Powhatans, exerting her influence among them. This was the sort of story that would be welcomed in London.

In his reports to the Supreme Council of the Virginia Company, Lord De La Warr did not dwell upon the difficulties and hardships of life in Jamestown nor upon Powhatan's War. He elaborated upon the friendship between the English and the Patawomekes and upon the great possibilities for settlement in the Potomac area:

> The last discovery during my continuall sickness, was by Captain Argall who hath found trade with Patamack (a King as great as Powhatan, who still remaynes our Enemie, though not able to do us hurt.) This [the Potomac] is a goodly River upon the borders thereof there are grown the goodliest trees for Masts, that may be found elsewhere in the World: Hempe better than English growing wilde in abundance: Mines of Antimonie and Leade without our Bay [Chesapeake] to the Northward. There is also found an excellent fishing banke of Codde, and Ling as good as can be eaten, and

of a kind that will keep a whole yeare, in shipp's hould, with little care; a tryall whereof I have brought over with mee.[7]

This glowing report was to become increasingly important to the managers of the Virginia Company. But for the Spelman rescue, Lord De La Warr would have had few encouraging words to carry back with him.

It was this growing concern with "public relations" that was to lead to Pocahontas' future contributions to the colonizing of Virginia. During the first three years she had made her contribution in a personal way, by assisting the settlers themselves. In the future her contribution was to be of a different order; she would become an ever more important instrument in a carefully outlined plan to unite the English and the Powhatans and to dramatize, and thereby promote, the Virginia Company's ambitious goal of establishing unchallenged claim to a part of the North American continent.

Pocahontas would not play her new role in the drama of Virginia until the stage could be set by the English—a task that would take almost two more years and involve the enlargement of the theater itself, as well as a strengthening of the cast of actors. However, by May, 1611, the Virginia Company had begun attending to these matters. In its second charter the company had prepared for the eventual extension of English holdings in the New World to include the territory two hundred miles north and south of Old Point Comfort, encompassing most of present-day Tidewater Virginia, Maryland, and Delaware, as well as a good part of North Carolina. The enlarged territory would increase the size of the colonizing area from ten thousand square miles to one million square miles. As the English saw it, in 1611 the task was not only to maintain the original settlement

[7] De La Warr, *Relation.*

on Jamestown Peninsula but also to enlarge as extensively and rapidly as possible the English commitment in America.

On May 19, 1611, Sir Thomas Dale arrived at Jamestown to assume temporary command of the colony, pending the arrival of the deputy governor, Sir Thomas Gates, later in the year. Dale, who was on a three-year leave of absence from military duties in the Low Countries, brought with him the skill and experience of a veteran military commander. More than any English leader in the colony before him, Dale erected in the Virginia wilderness an outpost of Old World civilization that could survive and prosper. Under his leadership the colonists would be able to meet all obstacles, including the militancy of Powhatan, with new and greater force.

From May 12 to May 19, 1611, Dale had supervised repairs at Fort Henry and Fort Charles, fortifications Lord De La Warr had built at the mouth of the James. Then he proceeded to Jamestown, relieved Percy of his interim command, and posted "for the publique view" the "Laws Devine, Morall, and Martiall"[8] established by the second charter but only now to be enforced within the colony. The laws were severe instruments of discipline (the colonists called them the "Laws of Blood") designed to strengthen the moral fiber of the colony and to make it an effective community. Among other things, the laws prohibited the use of profanity, the vilification of the Christian faith, and the belittlement of the king or of the officials of the Virginia Company. The first violation was to be punished by flogging; the second, by a bodkin thrust through the tongue; the third, by death.

Totalitarian rule had arrived at Jamestown, a rigid structuring of human lives that was necessary for the common good, according to the lights of the Virginia Company officials, who believed

[8] "The Copy of the Commission Granted to the Right Honourable Sir Thomas West (Knight), Lord De La Warr," Add. MS 21993, fol. 187; MS 12496, fol. 456, Department of Manuscripts, Library, British Museum.

that many of the failures in Jamestown could have been avoided if only the colonists themselves had been better prepared, spiritually and morally, to meet the inevitable hardships. The regulations designed to improve the "nature" of the colonists were also severe. The first time a man failed to attend church services without showing good cause he forfeited his week's allowance of food. The second time, he was soundly flogged. The third time, he was shot, hanged, or tied to a stake and burned. Desertion, theft, unauthorized harvesting of corn belonging to others, unauthorized picking of flowers, unauthorized gathering of grapes, unauthorized slaughtering of domestic animals—all these acts were offenses punishable by having one's ears cut off and being branded on the hand or by being forced to lie "head and heels together" all night. Refusal to accept a minister's spiritual advice was to be punished by flogging until the sinner either repented or died.[9]

Sir Thomas Dale enforced the laws vigorously. His goals were, first, to eliminate all idleness among the colonists and, second, to extend England's power beyond Jamestown. He attended to the idleness first. He wrote to the Supreme Council that, although the colonists kept their livestock in good condition, in Jamestown's fields he saw "no corn sett, some few seeds put into a private garden or two."[10] He began to work the colonists under the lash to get the fields planted before the hot, humid days of summer. He was convinced that military regimen was necessary to make the colony truly productive.

In his campaign to improve the colonists Dale was assisted by the Reverend Alexander Whitaker, a twenty-six-year-old friend and admirer who had left a prosperous parish in northern England to administer the Holy Sacraments of the Church of Eng-

[9] *Ibid.*
[10] Charles E. Hatch, Jr., *Jamestown, Virginia,* National Park Service *Historical Handbook Series No. 2,* 15.

land to the colonists and, he hoped, convert the Powhatans as well. Though Mr. Bucke was still principal minister at Jamestown, Mr. Whitaker was Dale's chief supporter, eager to serve "our religious and valiant Governour," whom he saw as "a man of great knowledge in Divinity, and of a good conscience in all his doings: both which Bee rare in a martial man."[11]

By June, 1611, Dale had imposed serenity and order on Jamestown and was ready to attend to his second goal, the establishment of a new town in Virginia. Dale's plan, approved by the Supreme Council in London, was to maintain Jamestown as a port of entry but to build the principal colonial settlement elsewhere. He set out in June in search of a townsite, leading an expedition by boat up the James River deep into Powhatan's country. The mission was a dangerous one, of course, and certainly William Strachey and the "Ancients"—as the original Jamestown settlers were now called—had warned Dale about the Powhatan menace. But Dale, who had not hesitated to yank Captain Newport's beard in public and threaten him with hanging,[12] was not one to be intimidated by savages.

Sailing up the James past the village of Apamatuks, which was governed by Queen Oppussoquionuske, Pocahontas' aunt, Dale selected a site for the new settlement about forty-five miles upstream from Jamestown on a high and healthful peninsula jutting out into the James like a great jaw. Dale studied the topography of the area with a keen military eye and planned how the defenses of the peninsula should be built. He decided that about seven acres at the point would have to be impaled, or enclosed in a stockade, and severed from the mainland. The

---

11 Raphe Hamor, *A True Discourse of the Present Estate of Virginia, and the Successe of the Affaires There till the 18 June, 1614* . . ., 59; hereafter cited as *A True Discourse.*

12 Newport had angered Dale by belittling Sir Thomas Smythe, treasurer of the Supreme Council.

town would be built on the point and fortified with five block-houses.

Dale returned to Jamestown and throughout the summer of 1611 kept the men at work felling trees for posts and lumber for the new buildings. He also saw to it that millwrights, lime burners, and bricklayers were kept busy. By the time Sir Thomas Gates arrived in the middle of September, 1611, Dale was ready to take 350 laborers and builders up the James to start construction of the new town, which was to be called Henrico in honor of Prince Henry, King James's oldest son and heir apparent. With characteristic military precision and energy Dale divided the workmen into two companies. One group, under the command of Captain Edward Brewster, would take the land route to the building site. The other group, under Dale's own command, would take the water route, escorting barges loaded with building supplies.

Evidence that Powhatan was still waging war soon presented itself, and on the trip to the new townsite Dale may well have gained some insight into the grievous problems that had beset the earlier colonists. Captain Brewster's men had scarcely set out when they were attacked by Chief Munetute, a minor Powhatan chief, and his warriors. The chief was grotesquely painted and wore on each shoulder the wing of a swan, a decoration that earned him the nickname "Jack of the Feathers" among the colonists. Munetute's warriors killed several of the colonists before they could reach for match and powder. Only after a fierce encounter were the colonists finally able to drive the Indians away with guns, poleaxes, and pikes and continue on the way.

Dale's group was also attacked, but more treacherously. Upon reaching the village of Apamatuks, twenty of his men accepted the invitation of Indian maidens to lay down their arms and spend the night. The invitation proved to be a trap. All twenty men were slain by order of Queen Oppussoquionuske, who, after the killings, appropriated the colonists' weapons.

The rest of the men made their way to Henrico safely and began building the new town, despite almost daily attacks by Powhatans. Dale first had the men impale seven acres at the point of the peninsula, a task they completed in ten days. Then he directed them in severing the impaled land from the mainland, using techniques he had learned in the Low Countries. The severed and impaled land, where Henrico was to be built, is today called Farrar's Island. The gap between the island and the mainland was named Dutch Gap, the name it still bears today.

Raphe Hamor, a recently arrived colonist, was an eyewitness to the construction of Henrico. Three years after its completion, while serving as the colony's secretary, he wrote the following description of the town:

> There is in the town three streets of well framed houses, a hansome Church, and the foundations of a more stately one laid, of Brick, in length an hundred foote, and fifty foot wide, besides store houses, watch-houses, and such like: there are also ornaments belonging to the towne, upon the verge of the river, five fair Block houses wherein live the honester sort of people, as the Farmers in England, and there keep continuall centinall for the townes security. About two miles from the towne into the Main, a pale of two miles in length, cut over from River to River, guarded likewise with severall Block-Houses with a great quantity of corn ground impaled.[13]

---

[13] Smith, *Generall Historie*, Book IV, 111. For other accounts of the founding of Henrico, see Robert Hunt Land, "Henrico and Its College," *William and Mary Quarterly*, 2d Ser., Vol. VIII, 464–68; The Rev. George J. Cleaveland, "The Reverend Alexander Whitaker, M.A. Parson of Henrico, Apostle to the Indians, a Saviour of Virginia," *Virginia Churchman*, Vol. LXVI, No. 2 (June, 1957), 16–17; The Rev. George J. Cleaveland, "The Beginning of a Good Work," *Virginia Churchman*, Vol. LXX, No. 6 (December, 1961), 12–14.

Henrico was completed around January 15, 1612, and its completion marked the beginning of a new era for the English. The town came to represent the expansionist mood of the English and of their determination to establish their new "nation" in the face of opposition from the French and the Spaniards. Even before Henrico was completed, Dale had revealed plans for still more towns in Virginia. On Christmas Day, 1611, he had burned to ashes Queen Oppussoquionuske's village—as punishment for the slaughter of his men—and had announced that he would build a town on the site of the razed village, to be called Bermuda Hundred.[14]

Indeed, signs of success were beginning to appear in Virginia. Dale's achievements were important steps forward; the friendship with the Patawomekes assured for the colonists a continuing supply of grain. There were soon to be further promising developments, among them a new and elaborate charter, to be issued the London Company on March 12, 1612. Soon the tobacco industry would be introduced into Virginia, to serve as the economic foundation of the expanding colony. Only one dark shadow hovered over English advances in the New World—Powhatan's War that continued month in and month out, year in and year out, always threatening the colonists with imminent danger and ultimate defeat. The English could not claim a real success until they had come to terms, one way or another, with the Powhatans.

[14] Strachey, *Historie*, Cap. VI, 73–78; McCary, *Indians in Seventeenth-Century Virginia*, 3.

CHAPTER XII

The Abduction and Conversion

WITH THE PROSPECTS NOW BRIGHT for permanent settlement in Virginia, serious efforts were made to resolve the Powhatan problem. In these efforts Pocahontas was to play a major part. For several years the English had contemplated capturing certain key Powhatans and using them as hostages to force Chief Powhatan to negotiate. Virginia Company officers had suggested one rather vague plan of abduction to Lord De La Warr:

> Yt is very expedient that your Lordship with all diligence endeavor the conversion of the natives and savages to the knowledge and

worship of the true God and their redeemer Christ Jesus as the most pius and noble end of this plantation, [which] the better to effect, you are to procure from them some of their Children to be brought up in our language and manners and if you think it necessary you first remove from them Quiacocks [quiyoughcosughes] or priests by a surprise of them and detayning them prisoners and in case they shall be wilful obstinate, then to send us some 3 or 4 of them into England, [so that] we may endeavor their conversion there.[1]

Perhaps abducting Indian children did not appeal to De La Warr, or perhaps he did not believe that converting three or four children and returning them to the Powhatans would necessarily transform the Indians into peaceful Christian neighbors. Whatever his objections, he ignored the plan, and no abductions took place.

Yet the idea lingered in colonial minds. The Virginia Company officials alluded to it in the Instructions, Orders, and Constitutions for the colony,[2] and the English clergy had supported the idea for some time, largely because of their interest in converting the Indians. In May, 1609, the Reverend William Symonds, preaching to Jamestown-bound colonists in Whitechapel, had ended his sermon by reminding his hearers that "a captive girl brought Naman to the Prophet. A captive woman was the means of converting Iberia. . . . God makes the weake things of the worlde confound the mighty, and getteth himselfe praise by the mouth of babes and sucklings."[3]

In one English mind in particular—that of Captain Samuel

---

[1] "The Copy of the Commission Granted to the Right Honourable Sir Thomas West (Knight), Lord De La Warr," Add. MS 21993, fol. 187; Add. MS 12496, fol. 456, Department of Manuscripts, Library, British Museum.

[2] *Ibid.*

[3] William Symonds, *A Sermon Preached at White-Chappel, in the Presence of Many Honourable and Worshipfull, the Adventurers and Planters for Virginia. 25 April, 1609* (photostat).

Frontispiece and title page of John Smith's *Generall Historie*, 1624.

141

John Smith as a prisoner of the Powhatans. From John Smith's *Generall Historie*, 1624. Top: "A Conjurer," "Their Idoll [Okeus]," "A Priest." Below: "Their Comunation [Conference] about John Smith 1609."

142

Smith taketh the King of Pamavnkee prisoner 1608

"John Smith taketh the King of Pamaunkee prisoner 1608."
From John Smith's *Generall Historie*, 1624.

Pocahontas rescues John Smith from Powhatan's warriors. From John Smith's *Generall Historie*, 1624. Top: "The countrey wee now call Virginia beginneth at Cape Henry distant from Roanoack 60 miles, where was S^r. Walter Raleigh's plantation and because the people differ very little from them of Powhatan in any thing, I have inserted those figures in this place because of the conveniency." Below: "King Powhatan comands J. Smith to be slayne, his daughter Pokahontas beggs his life his thankfullness and how he subjected 39 of their kings reade history."

144

Chief Powhatan's mantle, decorated with figures embroidered
in roanoke, which the chief gave to Captain Christopher Newport, to be presented to King James I. In the Ashmolean Museum, Oxford.

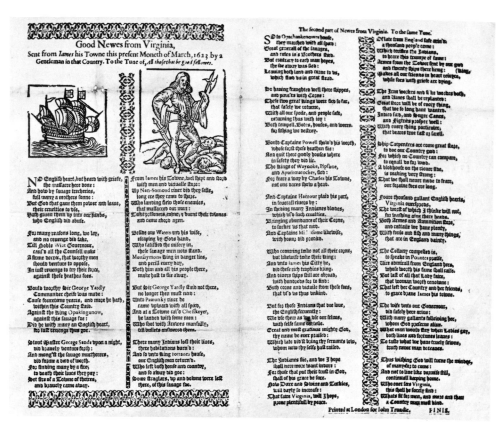

Broadside, "Good Newes from Virginia," sent to England in 1623.

Heacham Hall, the Rolfe manor house Pocahontas visited in 1616. In that year the house consisted of the central wing. The imposing wing at the left was added later. Heacham Hall was destroyed by fire in 1945.

St. George's Church, Gravesend, England, site of Pocahontas' burial in 1616.

Interior, new St. George's Church, Gravesend, England.

Statue of Pocahontas
in St. George's churchyard,
Gravesend, England.

Bas-relief of Pocahontas in the Church of St. Mary the
Virgin, Heacham, Norfolk, England.

Village road sign commemorating Pocahontas at Heacham, Norfolk, England.

Statue of Captain John Smith, Jamestown, Virginia.

Argall—the idea of an abduction took root, and in 1613 he acted on the idea, confident that his scheme would greatly strengthen the colonists' influence over Chief Powhatan.

Argall had returned to Virginia from England in June, 1612. He was encouraged by the progress that was being made in the colony: "I found both the countrey and people in farre better estate there."[4] Soon after his arrival he busied himself "helping to repaire such ships and Boats, as I found heere decayed for lack of Pitch and Tarre: and in pursuing the Indians with Sir Thomas Dale for their Corne, of which we got some quantitie, which we were like to have bought very deerely."[5] Argall also continued to explore the area and renewed his friendly contact with the Patawomekes. In December, 1612, he procured from them about eleven hundred bushels of corn.[6]

In April, 1613, Argall returned again to the Patawomekes' region, and it was on that visit that he decided to abduct Pocahontas, take her to Jamestown as a royal hostage, and then inform Powhatan that if he wanted her released he must agree to an enduring peace. The plot may have originated with Sir Thomas Gates and Sir Thomas Dale, both of whom were now living in Virginia, or perhaps even with London Company officials. At any rate, Argall was enthusiastic about the idea. He was resolved "to possess myself of her by any strategem that I could use."[7]

The abduction was a gamble. No one believed that Powhatan would end the war simply to rescue his daughter, even his favorite daughter. Yet her capture should serve to convince him that the English were now powerful enough to maintain the colony and determined to do so.

[4] In a letter to Master Nicholas Hawes. (Purchas, *Purchas His Pilgrimes*, IV, 1764).
[5] *Ibid.*
[6] *Ibid.*
[7] *Ibid.*, 1765.

While sailing up Potomac Creek, Argall learned from his Indian guides that Pocahontas was living in the region.[8] Then he launched his scheme:

> So soone as I came to an anchor before the Towne, I manned my Boate and sent on shore, for the King of Pastancy [Pasptanze] and Ensign Swift (whom I had left as a pledge of our love and truce, the Voyage before) who presently came and brought my pledge with him: Whom after I had received I brake the matter to this King, and told Him that if he did not betray Pokahuntis into my hands; wee would no longer be brothers nor friends.[9]

Argall's demand placed the chief of the Patawomekes in a difficult position:

> Hee alleaged, that if hee should undertake this businesse, then Powhatan would make warres upon him and his people; but upon my promise that I would joyne with him against him [Powhatan] hee . . . called his counsell together: and after some houres deliberation, concluded rather to deliver her into my hand, then [than] lose my friendship.[10]

According to Ensign Swift, who gave an eyewitness account of the affair to Raphe Hamor, the recorder at Henrico, the final details of the abduction were worked out with Captain Argall's special friend among the Patawomekes, one Jopassus (or Japazeus), his adopted "brother." Jopassus and his wife were won over to the plot by the promise of a copper kettle. Their role in the plot was to lure Pocahontas aboard the *Treasurer*, lying at anchor in the Potomac River, for what was ostensibly to be a tour of the ship.[11]

[8] Neill, *History of the Virginia Company*, 88–89.

[9] Purchas, *Purchas His Pilgrimes*, IV, 1765; Neill, *History of the Virginia Company*, 85.

[10] *Ibid.*

[11] *Ibid.*, 89–90.

Pocahontas was, of course, easy prey. She was "desirous to renue her familiarities with the English and delighting to see them would gladly visit...."[12] On April 13, Pocahontas, Jopassus, and his wife boarded a waiting shallop in a cove near the mouth of Potomac Creek[13] and were rowed to the *Treasurer*, where they were conducted on the promised tour and afterward entertained at dinner served in Argall's quarters.

After dinner Jopassus and his wife led Pocahontas into the gunners' room and left her there, pretending that they would soon return. Instead, carrying their copper kettle, they hurriedly left the ship, and Pocahontas soon discovered that she was Argall's prisoner—whereupon, reported Argall, she grew "pensive and discontented." Argall did not relent and "presently departed from Patawomeke it being the 13 of Aprill, and repayred with all speed to Sir T. Gates [at Jamestown] to know of him upon what condition he would conclude this peace and what he would demand: to whom I also delivered my prisoner."[14]

Word quickly spread throughout Jamestown and the new settlements, Henrico, Bermuda Hundred, and Elizabeth City, that the royal princess, the "delight and darling" of Powhatan, had returned. Though Pocahontas had not visited the English for three years, she was well known among them, and Ensign Swift reported that her fame had "even bin spred in England."[15] She received a royal welcome from the Ancients who had known her in the early days.

Pocahontas' appearance had probably changed but little in the years since the colonists had last seen her. She was a small,

[12] *Ibid.*

[13] See Stewart, "Excavating the Indian Village of Patawomeke," *Explorations and Field Work of the Smithsonian in 1938*, 87–90. By following Stewart's directions, one can easily find this site, as well as the spring under the bluff known to be the scene of Pocahontas' abduction.

[14] Neill, *History of the Virginia Company*, 87.

[15] *Ibid.*, 89–90.

graceful young woman with alert dark eyes elongated at the corners, and lovely, expressive hands.[16] Her long, dark hair streamed down her back, though at the sides and over her forehead it was now cut short, in the fashion of unmarried Powhatan girls. Gentle and outgoing by nature, yet she was every inch a princess.

Soon after Argall had delivered Pocahontas to Gates, "an Indian was dispatched to Powhatan to let him know, that I had taken his Daughter and if he would send home the Englishmen (whom he deteined in slaverie with such armes and tooles, as the Indians had gotten and stolen) and also a great quantitie of Corne that then he should have his Daughter restored, otherwise not."[17]

At first Chief Powhatan seemed willing to meet these conditions: "This newes much grieved this great King, yet without delay, he returned the messenger with this answer. That he desired me to use his Daughter well, and bring my ship into his River, and there he would give mee my demands; which being performed, I should deliver him his Daughter and we should be friends."[18]

At this point Captain Argall turned the negotiations over to Sir Thomas Gates and Sir Thomas Dale, the two highest-ranking colonists in Virginia. Gates and Dale tried to persuade Powhatan to release the prisoners, return the weapons, and supply the grain that Argall had demanded. They also hoped, no doubt, for a settlement of Powhatan's War. But, as might be expected, the chief was not easy to deal with. A few days after Pocahontas was taken prisoner, he sent back to Jamestown seven of the Englishmen he had held captive, but kept all the stolen English goods,

[16] Portraits of Pocahontas by various artists show her hands as particularly graceful.
[17] Neill, *History of the Virginia Company*, 86.
[18] *Ibid.*, 87.

except for a broadax and a long whipsaw. He sent only one canoeful of grain, though he promised to try to send more after the harvest. There were no indications that he had decided to stop fighting.

In fact, it soon became apparent that Powhatan was not going to respond further to Pocahontas' abduction. Knowing full well that she was safe and well cared for, Chief Powhatan simply let the seasons pass away—spring into summer, summer into autumn, autumn into winter—without sending so much as a message to Gates or Dale. If the colonists' strategy had been to move Powhatan's fatherly heart toward peace and reconciliation, Powhatan's strategy was to ignore the colonists altogether or patiently wait them out. Gates and Dale soon realized that if Pocahontas was to be used as pawn in their political chess game with the Indians, the abduction in itself was not going to produce checkmate. Several other moves would have to be made.

At some point in the succeeding months it occurred to Gates and Dale that Pocahontas could be useful to them in other ways, to the ultimate benefit of the colony.[19] Thus, while they waited hopefully for some positive response from Chief Powhatan, they

---

[19] Before the end of the summer of 1613 news of Pocahontas' capture had reached England. In a letter dated August 1, Sir John Chamberlain wrote Sir Dudley Carleton the following: "There is a ship come from Virginia, with news of their well-doing, which puts some life into that action. . . . They have taken a daughter of a King, that was their greatest enemy as she was going a feasting upon a river to visit certain friends; for whose ransome the father offers whatsoever is in his power, and to become their friend, and to bring them where they shall meet with gold mines. . . ." (Letter from John Chamberlain to Sir Dudley Carleton, August 1, 1613, MS 4173, "Bibliotheca Birchiana," Department of Manuscripts, Library, British Museum; Thomas Birch, *Court and Times of James I*, I, 262–63.) Chamberlain's letter exaggerates the ransom that Powhatan was willing to pay for Pocahontas, but the letter is an important demonstration of the attitude that the English were taking toward Pocahontas—that she was the golden key to a prosperous future in the New World and a symbol of success that would be worthy of English support. Her abduction did indeed put "some life into that action."

attended more or less deliberately to the transformation of Pocahontas into a "model Indian princess."

Pocahontas was placed in the care of the Reverend Alexander Whitaker, who took her to his farm near Henrico.[20] His women parishioners taught her to wear English dress, and he undertook the Pygmalion-like role of molding the young savage into an English lady. No longer was she permitted to offer sacrifices to Ahone at mealtime or repeat traditional Powhatan chants to the god. Whitaker taught her to bow her head and thank the Christian God for what she was about to receive. "Every Sabbath day," he wrote his cousin, the minister of Black Friars in London, "wee preach in the forenoon and Chatechize in the afternoon. Every Saturday night I exercise in Sir Thomas Dale's house. . . . Once every moneth wee have Communion, and once a year a solemn Fast."[21] Pocahontas was soon attending the services, and under Whitaker's tutelage and that of Sir Thomas Dale she became a student of the faith of the Church of England. "Her desire to be taught and instructed in the knowledge of God, her capablenesse of understanding, her aptness and willingness"[22] made her a receptive student. She also accepted, though at first probably with little understanding, the Prayer Book admonition to "renounce the devil and all his works, the vain pomp and glory of the world, with all covetous desires of the same, and the carnal desires of the flesh, so that thou wilt not follow, nor be led by them."

[20] Whitaker's one-hundred-acre glebe farm was selected by Gates and Dale as a suitable abode for Pocahontas because of its well-guarded location on impaled land about two miles from Henrico. Nearby were Forts Charatie, Mount Malady, Elizabeth, and Patience. Whitaker's house, "Rocke Hall," a frame house despite its name, was but a short distance from Mount Malady, where there was a sixty-bed hospital.

[21] Hamor, *A True Discourse*, 60.

[22] Letter from John Rolfe to Sir Thomas Dale, MS Ashmolean 830, fol. 118–19, Department of Western Manuscripts, Archives, Bodleian Library, Oxford University.

Unable to read or write English, though she could speak and understand a fair number of English words, Pocahontas memorized the Apostle's Creed, the Lord's Prayer, and the Ten Commandments, and learned the answers to the questions of the short catechism. With great effort she learned to recite other creeds and prayers, "which thing," Whitaker wrote, "Sir Thomas Dale had laboured a long time to ground in her."[23]

Finally, in the spring of 1614, Whitaker reviewed her in the catechism, received her renunciation of paganism, heard her confession of faith in Jesus Christ, and through the sacrament of baptism renamed her Rebecca and welcomed her into the fellowship of the Church of England.

In Pocahontas' conversion a major step had been taken in the colonists' efforts to influence Powhatan to accept the fact of English settlement and to display a Christian Indian woman as a symbol of the cultural blending of Old and New Worlds. Pocahontas' conversion also revealed much about her personality and character. It was indicative of her capacity for entering new arenas of experience. Whether or not she fully understood or accepted her new faith cannot be known. But in her willingness to learn English ways, English words, and English rituals, she revealed an extraordinary ability to move from a culture grounded in sacrifice and superstition into a culture that was by contrast enlightened and sophisticated.

23 Hamor, *A True Discourse*, 60; Purchas, *Purchas His Pilgrimes*, IV, 1770.

CHAPTER XIII

The Marriage

DURING THE TIME Pocahontas was held hostage in Henrico, she
became acquainted with a twenty-eight-year-old widower
named John Rolfe. Rolfe was an English gentleman, descendant
of a family that had come to England from Scandinavia long before the arrival of William the Conqueror. John was greatly
respected by his fellow countrymen both in Virginia and in his
native Norfolk County. He was a handsome man, a little above
medium height, with brownish hair streaked with gold, gray

eyes, and the short nose that was the distinguishing feature of the Rolfe family. He was well educated and may have attended Cambridge University.[1] Rolfe was the grandson of Eustace Rolfe, who in 1587–88 had contributed £25 (the equivalent today of £1,000) to help build the ships that defeated the Spanish Armada.[2]

John Rolfe, one of the survivors of the shipwreck in Bermuda, arrived in Virginia in 1610.[3] His primary concern was to establish the tobacco industry in the colony. He discovered that tobacco could be obtained in the New World only by buying it from the Indians or by cultivating it; the plant did not grow naturally or untended. Almost as soon as he arrived in Jamestown, he began experimenting with the cultivation of Spanish, English, and Indian varieties of tobacco, hoping to make the crop commercially feasible. In June, 1613, he shipped samples of his new "West Indian" tobacco back to England on the *Elizabeth*,

[1] Little is known about Rolfe's formal education. His writings indicate that he was well schooled. He may have studied with private tutors at his ancestral home, Heacham Hall, near King's Lynn, and later may have attended not-far-distant Cambridge University, where he would have absorbed some of the Puritan ideas reflected in the "conscience searching" letter he was later to write to Sir Thomas Dale. (A. E. Gunther, *The Rolfe Family Records*. 2–4, 200–202.)

[2] Rolfe had two younger brothers, Edward and Henry, both of whom remained in England. Edward settled in King's Lynn. Henry went to London, where he became a prosperous merchant and a member of the Virginia Company. After the death of Rolfe's father, his mother married Robert Redmayne, chancellor of the Diocese of Heacham. (Gunther, *The Rolfe Family Records*, 1–4.)

[3] In his report concerning the *Sea Venture* survivors in Bermuda, Sir Thomas Gates wrote: "We had the childe of one John Rolfe christened . . ., to which Captain Newport and myselfe were Witnesses, and aforesaid Mistress Hortan and we named it Bermuda." The Rolfe infant was shortly thereafter listed by Gates among those who died in Bermuda. (Purchas, *Purchas His Pilgrimes*, IV, 1746.) Whether the first Mrs. Rolfe died in childbirth, in Bermuda, or on the way to Jamestown is unknown.

and he was soon making regular shipments of more than one ton of high-grade tobacco to the English market.[4]

Soon after their meeting, Pocahontas and Rolfe began seeing one another regularly not only at church and at Mr. Whitaker's home but also in Rolfe's tobacco fields, where Pocahontas demonstrated for him Powhatan methods of growing tobacco. When the eighteen-year-old Pocahontas revealed to Rolfe her capacity for adapting to English ways of life, including the Christian faith, the lonely Rolfe began pondering the possibility of marriage to this young, attractive woman.

Early in 1614, shortly before Pocahontas became a communicant of the Church of England, John Rolfe composed a long letter to Sir Thomas Dale, in which he requested approval of the union from the English community, for he was aware of the impact such a marriage might have upon his own people.

In the letter Rolfe expressed his earnest desire to marry

> Pokanhuntas to whom my hartie and best thoughts are, and have for a long time been so intangled, and inthralled in so intricate a laborinth, that I was even awearied to unwind myselfe thereout. But Almighty God, who never faileth his, that truely invocate his holy name hath opened the gate, and led me by the hand that I might plainly see and discerne the safe paths wherein to tread.[5]

Rolfe admitted that the woman with whom he had fallen in love was

> one whose education has bin rude, her manners barbarous, her generation accursed, and so discrepant in all nurtriture from myself

[4] For a thorough discussion of John Rolfe and the Virginia tobacco industry see Melvin Herndon, *Tobacco in Colonial Virginia, "The Sovereign Remedy."*

[5] Letter from John Rolfe to Sir Thomas Dale, MS Ashmolean 830, fol. 118–19, Department of Western Manuscripts, Archives, Bodleian Library, Oxford University.

that oftentimes with feare and trembling I have ended my private controversie with this: surely these are wicked instigations, hatched by him who seeketh and delighteth in man's destruction; and so with fervent praiers to be ever perserved from such diabolical assaults (as I tooke those to be) I have taken some rest.[6]

Rolfe was clearly aware of the long-standing taboo against such alliances. He was not oblivious, he said, to the punishment meted out by God to the sons of "Levie and Israel" for marrying "strange wives." Notwithstanding, he sought Dale's permission for the marriage: "And did not my case proceede from an unspotted conscience, I should not dare to offer to your view and approved judgement these passions of my troubled soule." So that Dale would not believe that the proposed marriage was based solely on "desire of carnal affection," Rolfe declared that it would be for the "good of this plantation, for the honour of our countrie, for the glory of God."[7]

Dale was quick to agree that the marriage would be good for the colony, though he had probably never counted on the good fortune of such an event. It must have astonished all the Virginia Company officials that Rolfe, scion of an old and respected family, would be the one to propose such a marriage. Needless to say, Dale gave his prompt and wholehearted approval.

Emboldened by Dale's consent, Rolfe pressed his suit to Pocahontas, and to his joy she accepted him. Then Dale took charge of matters, using the forthcoming wedding as justification for attempting once again to press Chief Powhatan for a peaceful settlement of hostilities. Dale decided to return Pocahontas to her father and demand the ransom of any Englishmen still held as prisoners and the return of all English weapons. Then he would present Powhatan with news of the proposed marriage. which he hoped would persuade Powhatan to agree to peace.

[6] *Ibid.*   [7] *Ibid.*

In March, 1614, Dale, Rolfe, and Pocahontas, with an escort of 150 men, boarded the *Treasurer*, still captained by Argall, and sailed from Point Comfort to Werowocomoco, which Powhatan had once again made his capital. In Poetan Bay, Dale's men informed Powhatan's warriors that the English had come "to deliver up the daughter of Powhatan and receive the promised return of men and arms."[8] The Indians' response was several light forays against the colonists. Finally, with the *Treasurer's* guns and cannons trained on the four hundred Powhatans on shore, a small group of Englishmen landed and burned several Powhatan houses near the water's edge. Then a brief truce was declared while two of Pocahontas' brothers, delegated by Powhatan, went aboard the *Treasurer* to see how their sister "had been used" by the English. *Varobbie*

Pocahontas' appearance reassured the brothers. For her part, Pocahontas told them that she was deeply grieved by Powhatan's unwillingness to part with his English weapons in order to obtain her release, adding that because she had been so well treated by the English she intended to remain with them, now preferring them to her own people. Then Rolfe and another colonist, John Sparks, were sent ashore by Dale to negotiate with the chief himself. They were conducted not to the chief but to one of Powhatan's emissaries. Powhatan considered it beneath his dignity to negotiate with anyone but Dale himself.

Through the emissary, Rolfe and Sparks informed Powhatan about the proposed marriage. Much to their surprise, Powhatan sent back word that he gave his consent to the match and would be willing to make peace with the colonists. Rolfe and Sparks returned to the *Treasurer* with the good news. Though they returned without the ransom of all the white prisoners and the arms, there was general rejoicing over the chief's response. Rolfe and Pocahontas were no doubt pleased that the marriage would

[8] Neill, *History of the Virginia Company*, 90–91.

not offend Powhatan or arouse new hostilities. Dale was relieved by the prospect of peace at last with the Powhatans.

Ten days later, supposedly on the morning of April 5, 1614, John Rolfe and Pocahontas were married by Mr. Bucke, the senior minister in Virginia and a close friend of Rolfe's, in the little wild-flower-decorated church at Jamestown. Present at the wedding were Pocahontas' uncle Opitchapan, who gave her away, two of her brothers as Powhatan's representatives, and other guests, who had been summoned to the ceremony by church bells, whose chimes echoed pleasantly on the Jamestown air. The bride wore a "tunic of Dacca muslin, a flowing veil and long robe of rich material" from England. Encircling her neck was a chain of fresh-water pearls, a wedding gift from her father, who had refused to attend the ceremony.[9]

After their marriage John Rolfe and Pocahontas—now called Rebecca by the colonists—went to live in a house on the shore of the James River between Henrico and Bermuda Hundred. The land on which the house was built was another wedding gift from Powhatan. They called their new home "Varina," after a variety of tobacco that Rolfe had imported from Spain.

That the marriage symbolized for the colonists a lasting union between themselves and the New World was evident in comments Whitaker and Dale made shortly after the wedding. Whitaker wrote to his cousin in London: "Sir the Colony here is much better. Sir Thomas Dale . . . has now brought that to passe, which never before could be effected. For by warre upon our enemies, and kind usage of our friends, he hath brought them to seeke for peace of us, which is made, and they dare not breake."[10] Dale wrote to John King, the Bishop of London, that Pocahontas "is since married to an English gentleman of good understanding,

---

[9] Carolyn Thomas Foreman, *Indians Abroad*, 23; Smith, *Generall Historie*, Book IV, 113–14.

[10] Neill, *History of the Virginia Company*, 90–91.

and his letter to me contained the reason of his marriage to her. You may perceive another knot to bind the peace the stronger. Her father gave apprehension [consent] to it, and her uncle gave her to him in the church."[11]

There was an interesting confirmation that "another knot to bind the peace" had been tied. Dale, impressed by the Rolfes' compatibility and contentment, sent Raphe Hamor to Werowoc-omoco with an offer to "marry" Powhatan's youngest daughter. If Powhatan would consent to a union between Dale and the girl, then indeed "there could not be a truer assurance of peace and friendship."[12] But Powhatan told Hamor that he had already sold his youngest daughter "for two bushels of Rarwenoke"[13] to a great werowance "three daies journie from mee."[14] Pow-hatan evidently was not willing to give up another daughter to the English.

Then the chief asked about Pocahontas and Rolfe—"how they lived, loved, and liked." Hamor assured him that Pocahontas "was so contented she would not live again with him, whereat he laughed."[15] Most important, Powhatan confirmed the peace in a message he sent back with Hamor: "There have been too many of his [Dale's] men and mine slaine, and by my occasion there shall never be more . . . for I am now olde and would gladly end my daies in peace; if you offer me injurie, my countrie is large enough to goe from you. This much I hope will satisfie my brother."[16]

It was a message that the English had long awaited. And apparently Powhatan meant what he said. In the spring of 1614, seven years after the English had first arrived in Jamestown, the

[11] *Ibid.*, 92.
[12] Smith, *Generall Historie*, Book IV, 115.
[13] *Ibid.*, 116.
[14] *Ibid.*
[15] *Ibid.*
[16] *Ibid.*

struggle between the Powhatans and the colonists ceased. The marriage of Pocahontas and Rolfe did not herald a new day of mutual affection between Indians and Englishmen, and there would be isolated incidents of violence. But the English had established their foothold in the New World, and Chief Powhatan had at last recognized that he could not drive them away. The marriage of his daughter to an Englishman was a union he was not prepared to contest. Powhatan's War had come to an end.

CHAPTER XIV

A Matter of Money

Now THAT PEACE HAD DESCENDED upon Virginia, Sir Thomas Dale, Sir Thomas Gates, and other colonial leaders could turn to other vital matters, the most important of which was seeing to it that the colony was properly financed and adequately populated. The peace achieved with Powhatan presented a great opportunity to develop the colony to its fullest potential. Once again the English were to call upon Pocahontas to help assure Virginia's continued growth.

In 1615, Pocahontas gave birth to a son. Rolfe later wrote that the baby was the living image of his mother.[1] He was christened Thomas, possibly for Sir Thomas Dale. After his birth the Virginia Company, in appreciation of Pocahontas' many services to the colony, voted to provide an annual stipend for her and her son. To show its appreciation to John Rolfe, the company instructed Dale to appoint him recorder of the colony.

One important Englishman failed to share in the general enthusiasm over Rolfe's marriage. When King James was told of it, he was outraged and accused Rolfe of committing high treason in marrying the daughter of a savage king. James's Privy Council assured him that Rolfe's heirs would not inherit England's holdings in Virginia and further mollified him by reporting that the Chickahominies and other tribes in the Powhatan Confederacy were concluding separate peace treaties with Dale, who had promised each of eight Chickahominy chiefs a red coat or livery "from the King . . . [and] a picture of his majesty on copper, with a chain to hang around his neck." Thus bedecked, the chiefs were to be known as the "noblemen of King James I."[2] Reassured and flattered, James took a calmer view of events in Virginia.

James's reaction to the marriage was typical of the often irresponsible attitudes he had taken toward the colony and contributed to the problem of gaining the wholehearted support of the English people for the venture. James's unpredictability was a problem around which the colony's promoters had had to step cautiously for many years. He was an enigmatic man. On the one hand, he seemed to be fully aware of the importance of the Virginia colony and was eager to extend his domain beyond the seas and thereby become a more powerful Protestant monarch. On the other hand, he was quite capable of making overtures to

[1] Letter from John Rolfe to Sir Edwin Sandys, June 8, 1617, Box IX, Doc. 961, John Ferrar Papers, Department of Manuscripts, Library, Magdalene College, Cambridge University.

[2] Neill, *History of the Virginia Company*, 92.

Catholic Spain, which had consistently opposed England's colonial effort, with an eye to marrying his son Charles to the Spanish Infanta María. He could give his official blessing to the members of the Virginia Company and to their plans for Jamestown colonization and at the same time privately condemn the colonists for attempting to establish a Protestant colony in the face of papal bulls claiming the New World for Spain. He could be angered by the Rolfe marriage, seeing in it a threat to his "holdings" overseas, and at the same time be utterly indifferent to colonial affairs and refuse to become seriously committed to the success of the colonial experiment.

Moreover, James spent on frivolous causes money that could have been more usefully employed in support of colonization. He had inherited a debt of £400,000 from Queen Elizabeth, a debt which he could not discharge and over which he frequently quarreled with Parliament.[3] Yet he continued to spend great sums on inconsequential matters. Indeed, within five years of his coronation he had increased his debts to £700,000. Both he and his wife, Anne, spent money on elaborate masques and other frivolities, counting on replenishing their treasury through the marriages of their two sons and daughter to the wealthy offspring of European royalty.

In his indifference to the success of the Virginia colony, James hindered the efforts of both the clergy and the merchantmen. The planting of a Protestant colony was one of the most fervent wishes of such clergymen as Crashaw, Symonds, Donne, and John King, the Bishop of London, who were concerned with what they believed was their holy mission of converting the savages[4] and with saving the New World from Catholicism and

[3] William McElwee, *History of England*, 102–103; John Richard Green, *History of the English People*, II, 50.

[4] English clergymen were particularly stimulated to carry the faith to the New World when Mr. Whitaker sent to England an artificial toadstool (possibly

thereby putting a "bit" in their "ancient enemyes mouth."[5] The merchantmen, a comparatively new class in England, were searching for new markets and for cheaper and more abundant sources of raw material for home industries. Colonization of the New World was an obvious means of achieving those ends.

At length, realizing that no consistent backing would be forthcoming from James, a group of Virginia Company officers representing both clergy and merchantmen formed themselves into what became known as the Popular party, whose goal was to increase the company's capital and maintain its solvency. Among the members of the Popular party were Sir Edwin Sandys and the Earl of Southampton, Shakespeare's friend and patron. One of the tasks the party undertook was to collect monies already promised to the company (some stockholders had promised to "adventure" large sums of money in the Jamestown enterprise but had yet to honor their pledges[6]) and to encourage new investments.

Early in 1615 the group decided to hold a lottery in the churchyard of St. Paul's Cathedral, the proceeds from which were "to bring that work" in Virginia to a success as a "worthy Christian enterprise."[7] The lottery procedure was later described by the Reverend Samuel Purchas, the rector of St. Martin's:

> The great standing lottery was draine [drawn] in 1615 in the West end of Paul's churchyard . . . in which the Prizes were proportioned from two crowns (which was the least) to divers thousand . . . and

made of clay) painted in the image of Okeus as evidence of the Powhatans' pagan religion and their need of conversion.

5 Brown, *The Genesis of the United States*, I, Preface, xiv.

6 Neill, *History of the Virginia Company*, 84–85.

7 To gain support for the lottery, Sandys and his friends solicited the consent of the church officials at Canterbury and of the city's lay officials as well, knowing that as Canterbury went so went England. Accompanying a letter sent to Canterbury's mayor and aldermen by members of the Popular party were blank books in which to register the sums to be "adventured" by Canterbury citizens.

paid in money or in Plate there set forth in view, provided that if any chose money rather than Plate or goods for paiment in summes above ten crownes, he was to abate [rebate] the tenth part. The orders of this lottery were published, and courses taken to prevent fraud.[8]

The lottery was highly successful and encouraged the Popular party to devise an even more elaborate fund-raising project, based on an idea that had originated among clerics of the Church of England. These worthies had proposed that a school of religious instruction should be established in Virginia for both white and Indian children. The idea was put forth that the recently converted Mrs. John Rolfe might pay a visit to England to help launch the school. The possibility of such a visit had first been mentioned by Sir Thomas Dale in a letter to the Bishop of London.[9]

In 1616 the Virginia Company appropriated the idea as an opportunity to dramatize in a startling and colorful way the story of Virginia. By bringing to England the Powhatan princess who had become an English lady,[10] to be shown off to royalty, clergy, and merchantmen, the Virginia Company hoped to attract more money and more colonists to Virginia. In seventeenth-century public relations fashion, plans were made for Pocahontas to sit for a formal portrait. Ben Jonson would devise a court masque

[8] Purchas, *Purchas His Pilgrimes*, IV, 1773.

[9] Neill, *History of the Virginia Company*, 92.

[10] Pocahontas was not the first Indian woman to visit England. Ten years earlier, Captain George Weymouth had arrived with five Abnaki Indians from Maine. Among the Indians was a comely young woman who was given the name "Mrs. Penobscot" upon her arrival in England. Mrs. Penobscot made no lasting impression upon the English, however, even though she donned Elizabethan dress, was presented at court, and sat for a portrait. After all, Mrs. Penobscot was not a royal princess, nor had she achieved fame. (See A. L. Rowse, "The Elizabethans and America," *American Heritage*, Vol. X, No. 5 (August, 1959), 24–25.

for her entertainment. She would be received at court and be welcomed by the great people of the day.

And so, in the spring of her nineteenth or twentieth year, Pocahontas was called from her peaceful life at "Varina" to give her final and most colorful performance in the drama of American history.

CHAPTER XV

The Visit to England

On June 12, 1616, Pocahontas, her husband, her son, and a retinue of ten or twelve tribesmen and tribeswomen[1] arrived at Plymouth on the *Treasurer*. There she was met with pomp and ceremony by Sir Lewis Stukley, the Vice-Admiral of Devon, and other gold-braided officials. Escorted to London and housed at

---

[1] Among Pocahontas' retinue were her half-sister Matachanna, who was serving as young Thomas Rolfe's nurse; Matachanna's husband, Tomocomo, who painted his face and body and wore native dress—a decorated scalplock, a breechcloth ornamented with an animal's head and tail, and a fur mantle; another half-

the Bell Savage Inn on Ludgate Hill, Pocahontas began her visit, with all classes of English society prepared to pay her homage.

Virginia Company officials had made careful plans, designed "to advance the good of the plantation," calling for an enthusiastic welcome from the English people. The government would be represented by the king, the royal family, and the court; the church, by England's most distinguished divines; and the trades, by London's wealthy merchants and city companies. Her arrival was noted in a letter from John Chamberlain to Sir Dudley Carleton on June 22, 1616:

> Sir Thomas Dale is arrived from Virginia and brought with him some ten or twelve old and yonge of that countrie, among whom the most remarquable person is Poco-huntas (daughter of Pow-[h]atan a Kinge or Cacíque of that countrie . . . married to one Rolfe an English man.[2]

Perhaps the most important arrangements to be made were those for Pocahontas' presentation at court. The titled members of the Virginia Company, many of whom were not in royal favor, asked Captain John Smith to write a letter to Queen Anne calculated to interest her in receiving "Lady Rebecca." Though Smith was a commoner, he had dedicated his recently published *New*

sister; three Powhatan women servants, and four Powhatan men. The retinue had been organized by Sir Thomas Dale to enhance Pocahontas' status as a woman of royal birth.

Among those accompanying Pocahontas the most colorful was Tomocomo, who had been directed by Powhatan to count all the people he saw in England. As soon as he arrived at Plymouth, Tomocomo began making the count by notching a stick but soon abandoned the project because the people in England were as numerous, he later reported to Powhatan, "as the stars in the sky, the sand on English beaches, or the leaves on the trees." (Purchas, *Purchas His Pilgrimes*, IV, 1774.)

[2] Letter from John Chamberlain to Sir Dudley Carleton, June 22, 1616, Vol. LXXXVII, MS 375, State Papers Domestic James I, Public Record Office, London.

England Trials to Prince Charles, "the Most High and Excellent
. . . Prince of Wales . . . Heire to Great Britain, France and Ireland,"[3] and was at the moment in favor with the ruling family.

Respectfully addressed to "Most Admired Queene," Smith's
letter reviewed all the courtesies that Pocahontas had extended
to British subjects, including himself, since the founding of
Jamestown. He emphasized that if it had not been for Pocahontas "Virginia might [lie] as it was at our first arrival to this
day."[4] He described her "extraordinarie affection to our Nation,"
even after the onset of Powhatan's War terminated her visits to
Jamestown. He reviewed events of her life after her abduction
in 1613. Pocahontas, possessing far more wit and understanding
than others of her people, had rejected her barbarous condition,
and after accepting the Anglican faith

> had married an English Gentleman with whom at this present she
> is in England: the first Christian ever of that Nation, the first Vir-
> ginian ever spake English, or had a child in marriage by an English-
> man, a matter surely, if my meaning bee truly considered and well
> understood, worthy a Prince's understanding. . . . Thus most gra-
> cious Lady, I have related to Your Majestie what at your best leisure
> our approved Histories will account you at large and however this
> may be presented you from a more worthy pen, it cannot come
> from a more honest heart.[5]

In concluding his letter, Smith made bold to hint that if Pocahontas was not

> well received by Her Majesty her present love to us and Christi-
> anity might turn to such scorn and fury, as to divert all this good to

[3] Smith, *New England Trials*, C2. Charles, James's younger son, had become
heir apparent to the throne upon the death of Henry, the older brother, in 1612.
[4] Smith, *Generall Historie*, Book IV, 121–24.
[5] *Ibid.*

the worst of evil, where finding so great a Queene should do her some honor . . . would so ravish her dearest blood to effect that, Your Majestie and all the King's honest subjects most earnestly desires. And so I humbly kiss your Majestie's gracious hands.[6]   •

Smith's letter was hurriedly written and lacked grace,[7] but it apparently facilitated Pocahontas' presentation at court. Shortly after receiving it, Queen Anne selected Lord and Lady De La Warr to act as Pocahontas' social sponsors, to attend her at court, and to accompany her to state affairs and to the theater.

In the portrait painted of Pocahontas at the time of her presentation at court, she is shown wearing a mantle of red brocaded velvet richly ornamented with gold, possibly selected by Lady De La Warr. The dark underdress decorated with gold buttons is in keeping with the fashion of the day. In place of a ruff she wears an elaborate white lace whisk, or shoulder collar. In her right hand she holds a fan made of three ostrich feathers. Her dark, Stuart-style hat is richly banded with gold, giving the illusion of a coronet. Her hair is hidden beneath what appears to be a reddish-colored wig of the style popular among high-born Englishwomen of the day. Despite the wig and the English attire, however, Pocahontas retains her Indian appearance. Her smooth skin has the copperish tint of her people. Her high cheekbones, dark eyes, and Powhatan features are preserved, as are her dignity and royal bearing.[8]

[6] *Ibid.*

[7] Smith wrote the letter while engaged in organizing an expedition to New England—the fourth attempt he had made to colonize the area since his departure from Jamestown.

[8] The artist of the portrait is unknown. Engravings of the portrait were made by the distinguished artist Simon de Passe and circulated throughout London. Sir John Chamberlain received one of the engravings and sent it on to Sir Dudley Carleton with an accompanying letter dated March 29, 1617 (Old Style Calendar). The engravings, mere caricatures in comparison with the portrait itself, bore the following inscriptions in Latin and English: "Matoaka als Rebecka Filia

To Queen Anne and her ladies in waiting, Pocahontas' appearance and behavior were wholly acceptable. (It is possible that the Indian princess may have outshone the English queen in both qualities—which would not have been difficult, for, in the estimation of many, Queen Anne set a bad example for her subjects, being frivolous, vain, and too fond of spirits, as was the king, to suit the Puritan element of the time.)

After the presentation at court, the Virginia Company officials proceeded to display Lady Rebecca's virtues to the English people. John King, the Lord Bishop of London, entertained her at Lambeth Palace with pomp and festiveness that was, according to Samuel Purchas, a guest at the party, accorded no other lady of his acquaintance. Purchas later wrote that "Master Rolfe's wife did not only accustome herself to civilitie but carried herself as a Daughter of a King, and was accordingly respected not only by the great Virginia Company, which allowed provision for herself and her sonne, but of divers particular persons of Honour."[9]

When she was not being honored at affairs of state, Pocahontas received distinguished Englishmen at the Rolfes' quarters in the Bell Savage Inn. One such gentleman was Sir Walter Raleigh, whose presence at court was forbidden and who must thus meet the visitor privately.[10] Always the gallant, Raleigh knelt and kissed her hand, reputedly commenting afterward on his joy and good fortune in greeting so beautiful a princess.

Potentiss: Princ: Powhatani Imp: Virginiae"; "Aetatis suae 21. A°. 1616"; and "Matoaks als Rebecka daughter to the mighty Prince Powhatan Emperour of Attanoughkomouck als Virginia converted and baptized in the Christian faith, and Wife to the wor^h. Mr Tho: [John] Rolff."

[9] Purchas, *Purchas His Pilgrimes*, IV, 1774; Lucy Aiken, *Court of King James the First*, 334.

[10] Raleigh, freed from the Tower after a twelve-year imprisonment, was, with James's reluctant permission, preparing for an expedition to the West Indies.

Raleigh also escorted Pocahontas to the Tower of London to introduce her to his good friend, the Earl of Northumberland, the older brother of George Percy, whom, of course, Pocahontas had known in Jamestown.

Still a prisoner in the Tower, Northumberland, the Wizard Earl, was working among his crucibles, retorts, and other scientific apparatus when Pocahontas paid her visit. He invited her to leave with him the double-shell earrings that she was wearing so that he might reset them in silver rims.

Captain Percy himself visited Pocahontas at the inn, as did other early Jamestown settlers who were in England at the time. Another notable visitor was the poet and dramatist Ben Jonson, who, meeting Pocahontas in the inn parlor, questioned her rapidly for five minutes and then for the next forty-five minutes sat staring at her curiously until Pocahontas finally withdrew silently to her quarters upstairs, leaving Jonson to his bottle of sherry. Sir Thomas Dale, of course, visited the Rolfes regularly, though personal problems kept him from giving them his full attention,[11] and he left most of the details of their English visit in the hands of Sir Edwin Sandys and other titled members of the Virginia Company.

The reception at court, the gala affairs, and the visits from distinguished men were exciting new experiences for Pocahontas. But after a number of weeks the strain of the fast-paced, complex life took its toll of her health. Several times she was forced to bed with respiratory ailments. At length it was decided

[11] Upon his return to England in 1616 Dale found his wife, whom he had married shortly before his departure for Virginia in 1611, seriously ill, and he was heavily in debt. He showed little inclination to return to the New World and complained that he had no friends, money, or influence in England. Rolfe tried to help Dale by reporting to the king and to Sir Robert Rich that "Sir Thomas Dale's worth and name in managing the affairs of this Colony will outlast the standing of this plantation." (John Rolfe, "A True Relation of the State of Virginia by Mr. Rolfe," Box I, Doc. 208, Duke of Manchester Papers, Public Record Office, London.)

that the damp air of London did not agree with her, and the Rolfes moved to Brentford, a village about nine miles west of London where the Earl of Northumberland's handsome manor, Syon House, was situated. The Rolfes took quarters in the Brentford Inn, and slowly Pocahontas began to recuperate.

At Brentford she continued to receive a stream of courtiers, and it was there that she was reunited with Captain John Smith, whom she had not seen in eight years and whom until her arrival in England she had believed to be dead.[12] Upon seeing Smith at last, Pocahontas was at first too overcome with emotion to speak. According to Smith, "She turned about, obscured her face, as not seeming well contented; and in that humour with divers others we all left her two or three houres, repenting myself to have writ [the queen] she could speak English. But not long after that, she began to talk and remembered me well what courtesies she had done."[13]

At one point in their conversation she called Smith "father," a title he quickly rejected, explaining that he "durst not allow of that title, she being the daughter of a King." At this, "with well-set countenance," she spiritedly replied: " 'Were you not afraid to come into my father's Countrie, and caused feare in him and all of his people and feare you here I should call you father: I tell you I will, and you shall call mee childe, and so I will be for ever and ever your Countrieman.' "[14]

After the meeting ended, Smith wrote that "divers courtiers and others of my acquaintance [who] hath gone with me to see her generally concluded they did think God did have a great hand in her conversion, and they have seen many English ladies

[12] To ascertain whether Smith was dead or alive had been another commission given Tomocomo by Chief Powhatan, who had also commanded him to have Smith, if he was indeed alive, show him the English God and the English rulers, of whom Smith had so often spoken to the chief.

[13] Smith, *Generall Historie*, Book IV, 123.

[14] *Ibid.*, 121–23.

worse favored, proportioned, and behaviored."[15] Smith and Pocahontas never met again, but he was always to remember her as an important person in his life, and eight years later, in the Dedication of his *Generall Historie*, he gave her, "that blessed Pocahontas," equal listing with the "beautious Lady Tragabigzanda . . . the charitable Lady Callamata . . . and the good lady Madame Chanoyes" among the women who had most helped him in his lifetime.[16]

After Pocahontas had apparently recovered from her fatigue, she and her husband paid a visit to Heacham, the Rolfes' ancestral home. This visit was one of their own choosing and not a part of the Virginia Company's program. Rolfe felt the time was ripe to introduce "Lady Rebecca" and little Thomas to his family. Heacham was about a hundred miles from London, a week's journey by coach, on a route through Cambridge, Newmarket, Ely, and King's Lynn.

The Rolfe family's response to Pocahontas is unknown. The family records yield no information. The fact that the visit was made seems to indicate that it was a success. The appealing portrait of Pocahontas and her child (which later came to be known as the Sedgeford Hall Portrait) may have been painted at this time or from sketches made during the visit to Heacham. In the portrait mother and son are strikingly similar in features and expression. The eyes of both are dark and searching beneath their straight black brows. Pocahontas' hair hangs down her back. Her crimson bodice is embroidered with silver buttons and ornaments. Her skirt is olive green. She wears the double-shell earrings reset for her in silver by the Wizard Earl, and the pearls around her neck are presumably the wedding gift from her father. Her son, standing at her side, is dressed in frilled blouse and sashed breeches. His hand rests in his mother's.

[15] *Ibid.*
[16] *Ibid.*

The Heacham visit drew to an end, and Pocahontas and Rolfe returned to London, where Pocahontas again became a captive of the company. The officials, eager to display her as often as possible during her remaining weeks in England, were blind to her now obviously failing health. Many events were scheduled, one of which was Ben Jonson's Christmas masque performed on Twelfth Night at Whitehall in Pocahontas' honor. On January 18, 1616,[17] Sir Charles Chamberlain wrote his friend Sir Dudley Carleton: "On Twelfth Night there was a masque when the new made Earl [of Buckingham] and the Earl of Montgomery danced with the Queen. . . . The Virginian woman Pocahontas with her father counsellor [Tomocomo] have been with the King and graciously used, and both she and her assistant were pleased at the masque."[18] In the same letter Chamberlain announced the news that Pocahontas was soon to return to Virginia "though sore against her will, if the wind would about to send her away."[19]

Pocahontas' seven-month visit was drawing to a close. Her task was completed, or nearly so, and the company began making arrangements for the Rolfes' return to Virginia. In nearly every way Pocahontas' appearance had been a success. It had inspired Sir Thomas Smythe to promote a second and even more successful lottery in St. Paul's churchyard, which produced a great deal more money for financing the Virginia colony.[20] John Rolfe had seized the opportunity to support Sir Edwin Sandys, an enthusiastic backer of Virginia and a critic of the king's apathy, and also to write a tract entitled "A True Relation of the

[17] Old Style calendar.

[18] Letter from John Chamberlain to Sir Dudley Carleton, March 29, 1617 (Old Style Calendar), Vol. XC, MS 454, State Papers Domestic James I, Public Record Office, London.

[19] *Ibid.*

[20] The prizes in the second lottery were quite large: one of 4,500 crowns, two of 2,000 crowns, and four of 1,000 crowns, as well as numerous smaller consolation prizes. (Brown, *The Genesis of the United States*, I, 119.)

State of Virginia," addressed to the king, which invited prospective colonists to partake of the fruits of paradise in the virgin wilderness of Virginia, where every Englishman could "sit under his fig tree in safety, gathering and reaping his labors with much joy and comfort."[21] Moreover, the clergymen of London and environs had committed themselves to building a school at Henrico and had begun preaching sermons to that effect and taking up collections for the project throughout England.[22]

Pocahontas, her husband, her child, and her retinue had made real and tangible a distant world and had brought Virginia, and indeed the New World, nearer to the lives of Englishmen at home. They had turned many thoughts westward across the Atlantic to a land of new hope and incalculable opportunity.

[21] Rolfe, "A True Relation of the State of Virginia, by Mr. Rolfe," Box 1, Doc. 208, Duke of Manchester Papers, Public Record Office, London.

[22] Tomocomo had a part in eliciting church support for a religious school in Henrico. Fascinated by Tomocomo's barbarism, particularly in contrast to Pocahontas' gentility, the Reverend Samuel Purchas wrote to a fellow clergyman: "I have often conversed at my good friend's Master Doctor Goldstone's, where he [Tomocomo] was a frequent guest; and where I have both seen him dance his diabolical measures, and heard his discourse of his countrie, and religion, Sir Thos. Dale's man being the interpreter." Purchas described Tomocomo as "a blasphemer . . . preferring his God to ours because he taught them . . . to wear their Devill-lock at the left ear, . . . and [he] believed that this Okee or Devil had taught them their husbandry." (Purchas, *Purchas His Pilgrimes*, IV, 1874.)

CHAPTER XVI

Gravesend

POCAHONTAS, WITH HER HUSBAND, child, and escort, was booked to return to Virginia late in March, 1617, on the *George*, one of three ships scheduled to sail from Gravesend, at the mouth of the Thames. While she was waiting for the ship in Gravesend or shortly after she boarded the ship, Pocahontas became gravely ill, probably with pneumonia, or perhaps tuberculosis.[1] Rolfe,

[1] There is a tradition that when Pocahontas became ill she was staying in a small cottage at the foot of what is today Stone Street, in Gravesend, not far from the Thames.

184

aware for months of his young wife's declining health, was nevertheless unprepared for the possibility that she might die. In an effort to comfort her grieving husband, she reminded him that "all must die. 'Tis enough that the child liveth."[2] With those words Pocahontas died, in her twentieth year, far from home in an alien land.

Her body was prepared for burial, and on that same day, March 21, 1616 (Old Style Calendar), the funeral cortege wound its way up the hill to St. George's Parish Church, an ancient church standing near the water's edge. The Reverend Nicholas Frankwell, the rector of St. George's, met the procession at the entrance to the churchyard and escorted the coffin into the cold, damp, dimly lighted church. A medieval church of Saxon origin, St. George's had been stripped of its statuary in 1538 by order of the crown and converted into an Anglican church.[3] In this unlikely setting Pocahontas' funeral was held.

Attending the funeral with Rolfe and Pocahontas' retinue were Captain Argall, now deputy governor of Virginia and commander of the three ships that were scheduled to sail from Gravesend; Raphe Hamor; and the captain of the *Lizard*, another of the ships. In accordance with the custom of the parish at the time, the men sat with John Rolfe on one side of the church, and the women sat on the other.

Mr. Frankwell read from the Book of Common Prayer the traditional service for the burial of the dead. Afterward, Pocahontas was buried in the chancel of the church and Mr. Frankwell made the following entry in St. George's register: "1616 March 21. Rebecca Wrolfe, Wyffe of Thomas [John] Wrolfe Gent. a Virginia Lady Borne, was buried in ye Chancell."[4]

[2] Letter from John Rolfe to Sir Edwin Sandys, June 8, 1617, Box IX, Doc. 961, John Ferrar Papers, Department of Manuscripts, Library, Magdalene College, Cambridge University.

[3] Robert Heath Hiscock, *A History of the Parish Churches of Gravesend and the Burial Place of Princess Pocahontas*, 8–9, 12–13, 24–25.

[4] *Ibid.*, 24.

Captain Argall sent a message announcing her death to the Virginia Company in London.[5] On March 29, Sir John Chamberlain wrote to his friend Sir Dudley Carleton: "The Virginian woman whose picture I sent you died last week at Gravesend as she was returning home."[6] To those who did not know her well the death of Pocahontas was merely a matter of interest. However, to the Ancients who had been Pocahontas' first friends at Jamestown, her death was especially sad. Captain John Smith was said to have commented: "Poor little maid. I sorrowed much for her thus early death, and even now cannot think of it without grief, for I felt toward her as if she were mine own daughter."[7]

[5] Though Rolfe also signed the message, Argall evidently wrote it; it has the cold, matter-of-fact quality of his other writings. Rolfe was concerned with caring for his son, who was also ill, as was Matachanna, the nurse.

[6] Letter from John Chamberlain to Sir Dudley Carleton, March 29, 1617, Vol. XC, MS 454, State Papers Domestic James I, Public Record Office, London. (By the Old Style calendar the new year began on March 25.)

[7] Marguerite Stuart Quarles, *Pocahontas: Bright Stream Between Two Hills*, 29.

CHAPTER XVII

An Epilogue

In his writings Captain Smith was to help make Pocahontas famous beyond her time, and as the Virginia Company went on to develop from their colony a New World empire, many more writers and commentators began to tell the story of Pocahontas in various ways. Though death cut short Pocahontas' life and though she played her role in history for only ten years, she was not to be forgotten. Her death at Gravesend marked the beginning of her immortality.

Not long after Pocahontas' death John Rolfe returned to Virginia. He left his son, Thomas, with Sir Lewis Stukley at Plymouth, who in turn placed young Thomas in the care of his physician, Dr. Manouri. Rolfe had wanted to take Thomas back to Virginia with him, but "by the advise of Captain Argall, and divers who also foresaw the danger and knew the inconvenience hereof, I was persuaded to do what I did."[1] Thomas was later entrusted to the care of Rolfe's youngest brother, Henry, in London. Rolfe never saw his son again.

Soon after his return to Virginia, Rolfe sent word to Chief Powhatan of Pocahontas' death. Shortly thereafter, Powhatan turned over leadership of the Powhatan Confederacy to his brother Opitchapan and went to live with the Patawomekes, as far as possible from the English settlements. He died a year later, in April, 1618,[2] at which time the Powhatan peace with the English was reconfirmed by Powhatan's brothers and successors, Opitchapan and Opechancanough.

Rolfe reported to his good friend Sir Edwin Sandys that Pocahontas' death was "much lamented" in Virginia. He wrote also of the "good estate of the colony (God be thanked)" and of the firm peace it enjoyed. "All men," he wrote, "now cheerefully labor about their grounds, their harts and hands not ceasing. . . . English wheate, flaxseed distributed to most men by the Govrnr and is putt in the ground: nothing neglected, wch in any waies may be avayleable to advance [the] Company. The Cattle thrive and increase exceeding well, the ploughes yerely worke and

---

[1] Letter from John Rolfe to Sir Edwin Sandys, June 8, 1617, Box IX, Doc. 961, John Ferrar Papers, Department of Manuscripts, Library, Magdalene College, Cambridge University.

[2] Powhatan's death was reported by John Rolfe on June 15, 1618, and the Reverend Alexander Whitaker published the news in a tract, which Purchas included in *Purchas His Pilgrimes*. (See also Smith, *Travels and Works of Captain John Smith*, II, 539.)

oxen are plentyfull."³ There was also evidence that the Indians were willing "to Parte with their children"⁴ and allow them to join white children in attending the school that was soon to be founded at Henrico.

Rolfe was concerned about his son's future welfare. The Virginia Company's stipend to Pocahontas had been provided for her lifetime only. In his letter to Sandys, Rolfe asked that the stipend

> may not die [with] my wife, but contynue for her childe's advancement wch will the better inable myself and him hereafter to undertake and execute what may be comaunded and requyred from us. Thus refering himself to yor approved wisdom craving pardon for my boldness, desyring no longer to live, then when I shall cease from studying and indeavoring to bend my best strength to [persevere] in this action for the advancement of . . . God, King, and Cuntry.⁵

Rolfe found consolation for his sorrow in devoting himself to the prosperity of the colony. For the next several years he worked to develop the tobacco industry. By 1619 tobacco, Virginia's "golden weed," had become the mainstay of the economy. In 1619 he also served as a member of the first representative legislative assembly in America, and helped shape Virginia's growth into an orderly and productive colony.

The only real tragedy of those prosperous years occurred in 1622, when Opechancanough, who had succeeded his less warlike brother Opitchapan, led an uprising against the colonists. By then the English population was so large and powerful that In-

³ Letter from John Rolfe to Sir Edwin Sandys, June 8, 1617, Box IX, Doc. 961, John Ferrar Papers, Department of Manuscripts, Library, Magdalene College, Cambridge University.
⁴ *Ibid.*
⁵ *Ibid.*

dian opposition could not deter its growth, but in the uprising more than three hundred colonists were killed. One of them was John Rolfe.[6]

Thirteen years later, in 1635, Thomas Rolfe, now a young man of twenty, at last returned to Virginia, the land of his mother. The Powhatans had not forgotten that their royal princess had had a son who was in his own right a descendant of the Powhatan royal line. When Thomas arrived in Virginia, he found waiting for him not only "Varina," the plantation on which he was born, but also thousands of acres of land in the provinces originally inherited by his grandfather, Chief Powhatan.

As attested to by Surry County court records, "Mr. Thos. Rolfe" possessed "by Guifte of the Indian King"[7] about twelve hundred acres along the fertile south shore of the James River, the region commonly known as "Smith's Fort." His holdings in the area extended a mile or so inland from the high bluff along Gray's Creek directly opposite Jamestown. To make certain that there was no question about Thomas' ownership of the land, before his death John Rolfe had taken out a royal patent on it for his son.

Powhatan had also left Thomas hundreds of acres scattered elsewhere within a twenty-five-mile radius of Jamestown. More than four hundred acres were within the Chickahominies' boundaries and were adjacent to Fort James. In order to retain possession of the land, Thomas was required to maintain the fort for three years.[8]

[6] Christopher Brooke, *A Poem on the Late Massacre in Virginia*; Susan Myra Kingsbury (ed.), *The Records of the Virginia Company of London, 1607–1622*, III, 550–51.

[7] Ann Page Johns, *The Rolfe Property, Warren House, at "Smith's Fort Plantation," 1652–1935*, 8.

[8] According to the wording of Act II, October 5, 1646, of the Grand Assembly of Virginia: "And it is further enacted and granted, That Left. [Lieut.] Thomas Rolfe shall have and enjoy for himselfe and his heires forever Fort James alias

Thomas remained in Virginia the rest of his life, becoming, like his father, a tobacco planter. In 1641, Thomas petitioned the Virginia General Assembly for permission to visit his Indian kinsmen, mainly an aunt, "Cleopatre," and his formidable uncle, Opechancanough. Under ordinary circumstances colonists were forbidden by law to "speak or parley"[9] with the Powhatans, so strained had been relations between the English and the Indians since the 1622 massacre.[10]

Though Thomas visited among the Powhatans, he preferred English life and participated in colonial rather than Indian affairs. He married an Englishwoman, Jane Poythress, and from their union descended seven successive generations of educators, ministers, statesmen, and lawmakers, among whom were the Blairs, the Bollings, the Lewises, and the Randolphs. One of Thomas'—and therefore Pocahontas'—most distinguished descendants was John Randolph of Roanoke, who represented Virginia in the United States House of Representatives and in the United States Senate. Thus, through her son and his descendants, Pocahontas lived on in American history.

The people of England did not forget her contribution to New World colonization. The church in which she was buried is no

Chickahominy fort with foure hundred acres of land adjoyning to the same, with all houses and edifices belonging to the said forte. . . . Provided that he the said Left. Rolfe doe keepe and maintaine six men upon the place during the terme and time of three yeares, for which tyme he the said Lft. Rolfe for himselfe and the said sixe men are exempted from publique taxes." (William Waller Hening [ed.], *Statutes at Large: Being a Collection of All the Laws of Virginia from the First Session of the Legislature, in the Year 1619,* I, 327; hereafter cited as *Virginia Statutes at Large.*)

9 Act XLVI, February, 1631–32, of the Grand Assembly of Virginia: "All trade with the Savages prohibited, as well Publique as private." (Hening, *Virginia Statutes at Large,* I, 173.)

10 The colonists captured and executed Opechancanough on October 5, 1645, finally destroying the Powhatans' power in Tidewater Virginia. (Abbot, *A Virginia Chronology, 1585–1783,* 16–18.)

longer standing. In the present St. George's, built on the same site, is a memorial tablet placed in the chancel at the direction of the Reverend John H. Haslam, the rector of St. George's from 1892 to 1899. The inscription reads:

> This stone commemorates Princess Pocahontas or Metoaka daughter of the mighty American Indian Chief Powhattan. Gentle and humane, she was the friend of the earliest struggling English colonists whom she nobly rescued, protected, and helped.
>
> On her conversion to Christianity in 1613, she received in baptism the name Rebecca, and shortly afterwards became the wife of Thomas Rolfe, a settler in Virginia. She visited England with her husband in 1616, was graciously received by Queen Anne, wife of James I. In the twenty second year of her age she died at Gravesend, while preparing to revisit her native country, and was buried near this spot on March 21st 1617.[11]

A second memorial to Pocahontas was installed in St. George's in 1914, when two stained-glass windows were presented to the church by the Society of Colonial Dames of Virginia. The windows, dominated by the biblical figures of Ruth and Rebecca, also depict Pocahontas at the baptismal font and are bordered by plants and trees native to Virginia. On July 16, 1914, the windows were dedicated by the Bishop of Rochester in the presence of the American ambassador to Great Britain and visiting American Navy personnel.[12]

In the years during and after World War II, St. George's fell

---

[11] Hiscock, *A History of the Parish Churches of Gravesend and the Burial Place of Princess Pocahontas*, 25. Unfortunately, the error in referring to John Rolfe as "Thomas" was transferred from the church registry to the tablet in the chancel. The date given, 1617, is the New Style calendar date; by the Old Style calendar the year of Pocahontas' death was 1616. But since she died on March 21, the New Year (Old Style Calendar) was only four days away and was therefore referred to after March 25 as 1617.

[12] *Ibid.*, 25–26.

into disrepair, and in England and the United States a total of
£4,000 was raised for its restoration and preservation as a
memorial to Pocahontas and nondenominational chapel.[13] After
its restoration the church was reopened by Nancy, Lady Astor—
a descendant of Pocahontas—and the church was rededicated by
the Bishop of Rochester on November 1, 1952, All Saints Day.[14]

On October 5, 1958, England and America again joined in
paying tribute to Pocahontas when a bronze statue of Pocahontas, presented to St. George's Church by the people of Virginia, was unveiled in the churchyard by the Governor of
Virginia, John S. Battle. Dogwood trees, representing the Virginia state tree, were planted in the churchyard by Governor
Battle, assisted by the Mayor of Gravesend, Councillor L. Kempster; Lord Hailsham, Lord President of the Council; the Bishop
of Rochester; and Lord Cornwallis, Lord Lieutenant of Kent.[15]

Elsewhere in England there are other memorials to Pocahontas. One is to be found in the Church of St. Mary the Virgin
at Heacham, the church which members of the Rolfe family
have attended since the sixteenth century. The memorial, carved
in alabaster, is the work of Ottillea Wallace, a pupil of Rodin.
According to A. E. Gunther, the memorial "takes the form of a
bas-relief from a portrait of the Princess . . . showing the lady
in the dress in which she attended Queen Anne of Denmark,
consort of James I, at a masque."[16] Conceived and planned by
Mrs. Charles Torrey (nee Neville Rolfe), whose husband was
an American by birth, the memorial was unveiled on May 27,
1933, by the Lord Fermoy, M.P., and was dedicated by the
Archdeacon of Lynn in the presence of representatives of the
Rolfe family and of Americans descended from Thomas Rolfe.[17]

[13] *Ibid.*, 25–29.
[14] *Ibid.*, 25–26.
[15] *Ibid.*, 29.
[16] Gunther, *The Rolfe Family Records*, 89.
[17] *Ibid.*

At the request of Mrs. Torrey the memorial was placed in the north aisle of the church directly above the bronze memorial to John Rolfe's father.

Also in commemoration of Pocahontas' relationship with the Rolfes, in 1960 the Parish Council of Heacham erected a village road sign that

> depicts a relief in wood of Princess Pocahontas supported by a Norfolk hackney and by a seahorse. The ground shows the industries of Heacham in lavender, shellfish, and agriculture. An inscription on an oak support eight feet high, built into a brick and carstone base reads as follows:

> THIS SIGN WAS ERECTED BY PUBLIC SUBSCRIPTION
> 9TH APRIL 1960
> COMMEMORATING PRINCESS POCAHONTAS
> THE INDIAN PRINCESS
> WHO MARRIED JOHN ROLFE
> OF HEACHAM MANOR
> ALSO DEPICTING PAST AND PRESENT INDUSTRIES.[18]

In the United States, too, memorials have been erected to Pocahontas. Over the western rotunda of the Capitol in Washington is a marble frieze depicting Pocahontas' rescue of John Smith. At Jamestown stands a bronze statue of her, evidently a duplicate of the statue in St. George's churchyard at Gravesend. As recently as 1964 an exhibit was held at Jamestown of articles that Pocahontas once touched or wore, such as the white double-shell earrings that the Earl of Northumberland reset for her and an exquisite little sewing basket made of gaily dyed porcupine quills.

Because of the intrinsically romantic events of her life, Poca-

[18] *Ibid.*, 92.

194

hontas has been made the heroine of countless sentimental stories, plays, and poems that have had the unfortunate effect of making her seem more a figure of legend than one of history. Yet it is her true story, lived in a critical moment of history, that gives her enduring significance—the true story that took place many years ago, when the American adventure began.

Bibliography

I. MANUSCRIPT MATERIALS

Department of Western Manuscripts, Archives,
Bodleian Library, Oxford University

Descriptive Analytical and Critical Catalogus Codd. MSS Bibl. Bodl., XIV and XIX, Oxford MDCCC.
Letter from John Rolfe to Sir Thomas Dale, MS Ashmolean 830, fol. 118–19. (Physical description [p. 491]: "This seems to be a copy.

196

It is fairly written on two first leaves of two sheets and is neither dated, directed, nor indorsed. It is addressed to an English gentleman in the time of James I." The text of the letter is Rolfe's profession of love for and intent to marry Pocahontas.)

MS Tanneri, CLXVIII, fol. 2. (Handwritten MS arguing England's right to found a colony in the New World.)

Department of Manuscripts, Library, British Museum

Birch, Thomas. "Bibliotheca Birchiana" (Birch's MSS), MS 4173. (Relates to unpublished manuscript correspondence between John Chamberlain and Sir Dudley Carleton [1616–17] coincident with Pocahontas' visit to England. Utilized both by Thomas Birch, in *Court and Times of James I*, and by John Nichols, in *The Progresses, Processions and Magnificent Festivities of King James I . . . .*)

"Instructions Orders and Constitutions by Way of Advice Set Downe Declared by and Propounded to Sir Thomas Gates (Knight) Governour of the Virginia Colony Therein Planted . . .: Given by Virtue of His Majesty's Two Patents . . . ." 35 pp. (Included are "The Copy of the Commission Granted to the Right Honourable Sir Thomas West [Knight], Lord De La Warr," and "A Coppy of Old Instructions Given to Sir Thomas Gates Now Given to Lord La Warre Signed by 'A Constant and Perpetuall Servant Thomas Dale 9th August 1611,' " Add. MS 21993, fol. 187; Add. MS 12496, fol. 456).

Strachey, William. "The First Booke of the Historie of Travaile into Virginia Britania Expressing the Cosmographie and Commodities of the Country Together with the Manners and Customes of the People Gathered & Observed as Well by Those Who Went First Thither as Collected by William Strachey Gent: 3 Years Employed Secretarie State and of Counsaile with the Right Honorable the Lord LaWarre His Majesty's Lord Governour and Captain Generall of the Colony," Sloane Collection, MS 1622.

White, John. American Drawings (originals), Roy. 18 A XI. Box 1: Title and 4–8, 10–19; Box 2: 20–24, 30–31, 37–43; Box 3: 44–59. Department of Royal Manuscripts.

Pocahontas

John Ferrar Papers, Department of Manuscripts, Library,
Magdalene College, Cambridge University

Letter from John Rolfe to Sir Edwin Sandys, June 8, 1617, Box IX, Doc. 961. (Apprises Sandys of Pocahontas' death and of Rolfe's decision to leave his son at Plymouth with Sir Lewis Stukley and also gives a description of the colony upon Rolfe's return to Virginia.)

Letter from George Thorpe to John Ferrar, 1621, MS 1019, Box X. (Urges Ferrar to have colonists examined by a physician before they embark for Virginia: "Of those few boys assigned to my oversight there are two that are so diseased . . . that one of them confessed he hath had [name of disease cut out of letter].")

Letter from William Turner to John Covett, December 20, 1606, Box X. (Gives details of delayed sailing of the *Susan Constant, the Godspeed,* and the *Discovery.* Difficult to decipher, it is the oldest letter pertaining to Virginia in the Ferrar Papers. It may have been deliberately vague in order to mislead Spanish spies whose duty it was to note dates of departure and return of ships to and from Virginia.)

Letter 1 to Sir Edwin Sandys (signature and date illegible), Miscellaneous Papers, Box XVI. (Relates to the making of iron. In the same folder is an undated, unsigned letter referring to Sir Thomas Gates and Sir Thomas Dale and to "the savages, and God.")

Letters from Sir George Yeardlye to Sir Edwin Sandys, 1249, imperfect, n.d.; 1250, July 20, 1619; 1251, June 7, 1620; 1252, May 11, 1621. Box XII. (Relate to Virginia colony.)

Public Record Office, London

"Grant to John Smith [of] 12d per Diem for Life (November, 19, 1616)," Grant Book, Vol. LXXXIX, MS 217.

Letter from John Chamberlain to Sir Dudley Carleton, June 22, 1616, State Papers Domestic James I, Vol. LXXXVII, MS 375.

Letter from John Chamberlain to Sir Dudley Carleton, January 18, 1617 (1616 Old Style calendar), State Papers Domestic James I, Vol. XC, MS 428.

Letter from John Chamberlain to Sir Dudley Carleton, March 29, 1617

(1616 Old Style calendar), State Papers Domestic James I, Vol. XC, MS 454.

Letter from Thomas De La Warr to Salisbury, June 3, 1611, State Papers Domestic James I, Vol. LXIV, 518.

Petition from George Yeardlye, George Thorpe, Sam Maycock, John Pory, John Rolfe, and other colonists to James I, January 21, 1620, Box 2, Doc. 290, Duke of Manchester Papers (classified under National Register of Archives). (Petitions James I to withdraw his "late proclamation" prohibiting the importation of tobacco into England.)

"A True Relation of the State of Virginia by Mr. Rolfe ni[nth] May, 1616," Box 1, Doc. 208, Duke of Manchester Papers. (One of three handwritten copies of a report concerning the Virginia colony by John Rolfe, recorder, addressed to "Ye right Hoble and Virtuous K^t Sir Robert Riche my singular good friend.")

Library of Congress, Archives and Photoduplication Service, Washington

"Early Records of Virginia," Safe 13. 2 vols. (Notes collected by Susan Myra Kingsbury, ed., for *The Records of the Virginia Company of London 1607–1622.*) Includes folio with Instructions to Colonists.

Virginia Miscellaneous (1606–1772), Box I. (Contains photostat of burial record of "Rebecca Wroth [Rolfe]," in St. George's Register, Gravesend, England.)

Microfilm copies of manuscripts, Dukes of Northumberland. Library (Alnwick Castle), British MS Project, as classified by Lester K. Born. Aln 114/5 (containing "Bill for Necessaries Bought by Mr. George Percy for His Voyage to the West Indies"); Aln 3/2 (F240) (Letters and Papers, 1600–1607); Aln 4/1 (F241) (Papers Relating to Military Affairs); Aln 4/2 (F241) (Letters and Papers, 1608–11, containing information about expenditures of George Percy and the payment by the Earl of debts incurred by Percy for clothing from London merchants); Aln 5/1 (F245) (Book of His Majesty's Offices, 1617, alluding to the tax of £30,000 levied on the Earl of Northumberland and his subsequent imprisonment in the Tower of London by order of James I for his alleged participation in the Gunpowder Plot).

Pamunkey Indian Reservation, King William County, Virginia

Cook, Tecumseh D. "Facts about the History of the Pamunkey Indian Tribe." Unpublished manuscript.

Varina-on-the-James, Richmond, Virginia

Stoneman, Janet Chase. "A History of Varina-on-the-James." Farmville, Va., Longwood College. Unpublished theme, 1957.

University of Pennsylvania, Philadelphia

Forman, Henry Chandlee. "Jamestown and St. Mary's Buried Cities of Romance." Unpublished Ph.D. dissertation, 1938.

II. UNITED STATES GOVERNMENT PUBLICATIONS, DOCUMENTS, AND RECORDS

Congress, House of Representatives. 82 Cong., 2 sess., *House Report No. 2503*, Ser. 11583.

Cotter, John L. *Archeological Excavations at Jamestown.* National Park Service *Archeological Research Series No. 4.* Washington, U.S. Government Printing Office, 1958.

Hatch, Charles E., Jr. *Jamestown, Virginia.* National Park Service *Historical Handbook Series No. 2.* Washington, U.S. Government Printing Office, 1957.

Hening, William Waller, ed. *Statutes at Large: Being a Collection of All the Laws of Virginia from the First Session of the Legislature, in the Year 1619.* 13 vols. New York, printed by the editor, 1819–23.

Hodge, Frederick Webb, ed. *Handbook of American Indians North of Mexico.* Bureau of American Ethnology *Bulletin 30.* 2 pts. Washington, U.S. Government Printing Office, 1907, 1910.

Holmes, William Henry. *Aboriginal Pottery of the Eastern United States.* Bureau of American Ethnology *Report 20.* Washington, U.S. Government Printing Office, 1903.

Index to the Writings on American History. Washington, U.S. Government Printing Office, 1956.

Kingsbury, Susan Myra, ed. *The Records of the Virginia Company of London 1607–1622.* 4 vols. Washington, U.S. Government Printing Office, 1906–35.

Lane, W. C., and N. E. Browne, eds. *Portrait Index.* Washington, U.S. Government Printing Office, 1906.

Swanton, John R. *The Indians of the Southeastern United States.* Bureau of American Ethnology *Bulletin 137.* Washington, U.S. Government Printing Office, 1902.

III. PRINTED PRIMARY SOURCES

Anonymous. *Good Newes from Virginia Sent from James His Towne This Present Month of March, 1623 by a Gentleman in That Country. To the Tune of, All Those That Be Good Fellowes. A Broadside Ballad from Virginia.* London, John Trundle, 1623. (Description: "This broadside ballad appears to be otherwise unknown; it is not recorded in *Short Title Catalogue,* Bishop, Sabin, Hazlett, B. A., Britwell or Bib Lindes *Catalogue of a Collection of Printed Broadsides in the Possession of The Society of Antiquitaries of London,* 1866." It antedates Anne Bradstreet's poetry and has the distinction of being the first poem written by an Englishman in the New World, since Christopher Brooke never visited America.)

Brinton, Daniel G., ed. *The Lenape and Their Legends, with the Complete Text and Symbols of the Walum Olum.* Philadelphia, 1885.

Brooke, Christopher. *A Poem on the Late Massacre in Virginia.* London, "Imprinted at London by G. Eld, for Robert Mylbourne and to be sold at his shop at the great South doore of Paul's [churchyard]," 1622. (From the Library of Lord Cromwell, Sprotborough Hall, Dorcaster, England, now in the Archives of the Thomas E. Gilcrease Museum of History and Art, Tulsa.)

Bry, Théodore de. *Historia Americae Sive Novi Orbis . . . ,* Frankfurt, Matthew Meriani, 1590–1634.

Cotes, Richard. *James I, King of Great Britain.* London, Michael Sparkes, 1651.

De La Warr, Thomas. *The Relation of the Right Honourable the Lord*

De La Warre, Lord Governour and Captaine Generall of the Colonie Planted in Virginia. London, William Hall for William Welbie, 1611. (Photostat.)

Eburne, Richard. *A Plain Pathway to Plantations.* Ed. by Louis B. Wright. Ithaca, Cornell University Press, 1962. (Originally published in London in 1624.)

Gray, Robert. *A Good Speed to Virginia.* London, 1609.

Gunther, A. E. *A Guide to Heacham: Its History and Architecture.* Heacham, Norfolk, June, 1963.

———. *The Rolfe Family Records.* Vols. I and III in one volume. Heacham, Norfolk, and London, Litho Developments, Ltd., 1962.

Gunther, R. T., and A. Gunther. *The Rolfe Family Records.* Vol. II. Heacham, London, and Aylesbury, privately printed, 1914.

Hall, Joseph. *The Discovery of the New World.* London, for Ed. Blount and W. Barrett, 1609.

Hamor, Raphe. *A True Discourse of the Present Estate of Virginia, and the Successe of the Affaires There till the 18 June, 1614 . . .* , London, "John Beale for William Welby dwelling at the signe of the Swanne in Paul's Church-yard," 1615. (Copy.)

Hariot, Thomas. *A Briefe and True Report of the New Found Land of Virginia.* London, 1588. (Description inside book: "A brief and true report of the new-found land of Virginia of the commodities and of the nature and manners of the naturall inhabitants. Discovered by the English Colony there seated by Sir Richard Grenville Knight in the yeere 1585 which Remained under the government of twelve moneths. At the Speciall charge and direction of the Honourable Sir Walter Raleigh Knight lord Warden of the Stanneries who therein hath been authorised by Her Majestie and her letters patents; This forebooke Is Made in English by Thomas Hariot, Servant to the above named Sir Walter, a member of the Colony. . . .")

Ingleby, Clement. *A Guide to the Rolfe Portraits, Formerly at Sedgeford Hall, Now Permanently in the Custody of the Urban District Council of Hunstanton.* Hunstanton, Witley Press, 1955.

Lorant, Stephen, ed. *The New World: The First Pictures of America Made by John White and Jaques Le Moyne and Engraved by*

*Théodore de Bry with Contemporary Narratives of the Huguenots'
Settlement in Florida 1562–65 and the Virginia Colony 1585–90.*
New York, Duell, Sloane & Pearce, 1946.

Percy, George. *Observations Gathered out of "A Discourse of the
Plantation of the Southern Colony in Virginia by the English, 1606."*
Ed. by David B. Quinn. Charlottesville, University Press of Virginia,
1967.

Purchas, Samuel. *Purchas His Pilgrimes.* 4 vols. London, William
Stansbury for Henry Fetherstone, 1625.

Rich, R. *Newes from Virginia* (poem). New York, Scholars' Facsimi-
lies & Reprints, 1937. (Originally published in London in 1610.)

Rolfe, John. *A True Relation of the State of Virginia Left by Sir
Thomas Dale.* New Haven, Yale University Press, 1951. (Originally
published in London in 1616.)

Smith, John. *Advertisements for the Unexperienced Planters of New
England or Anywhere: Or, the Path-Way to Experience to Erect a
Plantation.* London, John Haviland, 1631.

—. *The Generall Historie of Virginia, New-England, and the Summer Isles . . . .* London, printed by J. Dawson and J. Haviland for
Michael Sparkes, 1624.

———. *A Map of Virginia. With a Description of the Countrey, the
Commodities, People, Government and Religion. Written by Cap-
taine John Smith Sometimes Governour of the Countrey, Where-
unto Is Annexed the Proceedings of Those Colonies, Since Their
First Departure from England, with the Discourses, Orations, and
All Their Relations with the Salvages, and the Accidents That Be-
fell Them in All Their Journies and Discoveries.* Oxford, Joseph
Barnes, 1612. (Photostat.)

———. *New England Trials.* 2d ed. London, W. Jones, 1622.

———. *The True Travels, Adventures, and Observations of Captaine
John Smith, in Europe, Asia, Affrica, and America, from Anno
Domini 1593 to 1630.* London, "Printed by F. H. for Thomas Slater,
and are to bee sold at the Blew Bible in Greene Arbour," 1630.

Strachey, William. *Historie of Travaile into Virginia Britannia.* Ed. by
R. L. Major. Ser. I, Vol. VI. London, Hakluyt Society, 1849.

Symonds, William. *A Sermon Preached at White-Chappel, in the Presence of Many Honourable and Worshipfull, the Adventurers and Planters for Virginia. 25 April, 1609.* London, I. Windet, for Eleazer Edgar and William Welby, 1609. (Photostat.)

Wecheli, Joannis, and Théodore de Bry. *The American Indian as Depicted in a Collection of Plates Engraved by Théodore de Bry in the Year 1590; India Occident 1590–1602.* (A rebound volume of original De Bry engravings. Exact publication date unknown.)

Whitaker, Alexander. *Good Newes from Virginia.* Scholars' Facsimiles & Reprints, New York, 1937. (Originally printed in London in 1613.)

IV. BOOKS

Agar, Ben. *King James I King of Great Britain: His Apophthegmes or Table Talk.* London, printed by B. W., 1643.

Aiken, Lucy. *Court of King James the First.* 2 vols. London, 1822.

The American Heritage Book of Indians. New York, American Heritage Publishing Company, Inc., 1961.

America's Historylands. New ed. Washington, National Geographic Society, 1967.

Anonymous (*"By the Author of The Secret History of King Charles I and King James II"*). *The Secret History of King James I and King Charles I.* London, 1650.

Bancroft, George. *History of the United States.* Last rev. 5 vols. Boston, 1882.

Barbour, Philip L. *The Three Worlds of Captain John Smith.* Boston, Houghton Mifflin Company, 1964.

The Beauty of Britain. Intro. by J. B. Priestly. Rev. ed. London, B. T. Batsford, Ltd., 1962.

Bell, Adrian, George A. Birmingham, Edmund Blunden, Ivor Brown, Charles Bradley Ford, R. H. Mottram, and G. M. Young. *England's Heritage.* London, B. T. Batsford, Ltd., 1961.

Bemiss, S. M. *Ancient Adventurers.* Richmond, Va., Garrett & Massie, Inc., 1959.

Birch, Thomas. *Court & Times of James I.* 2 vols. London, Henry Colburn, 1849.

Bolton, Herbert Eugene. *Bolton and the Spanish Borderlands.* Ed. and with an introduction by John Francis Bannon. Norman, University of Oklahoma Press, 1964.

————, and Marshall Thomas Mailand. *The Colonization of North America, 1492–1783.* New York, 1920.

Brebner, J. Bartlett. *The Explorers of North America, 1492–1806.* London, 1933.

Brown, Alexander. *The Genesis of the United States.* 2 vols. Boston, Houghton Mifflin Company, 1890.

Burk, John. *The History of Virginia.* 4 vols. Petersburg, Va., Dickson and Pescud, 1822.

Chatterton, Edward Keble. *Captain John Smith.* New York, Harper & Brothers, 1927.

Churchill, Winston. *The New World (1485–1688).* Vol. II in *A History of the English-speaking Peoples.* 4 vols. New York, Dodd, Mead & Company, Inc., 1956.

Chute, Marchette. *Shakespeare of London.* New York, E. P. Dutton & Co., Inc., 1949.

Cotterill, R. S. *The Southern Indians: The Story of the Civilized Tribes Before Removal.* Norman, University of Oklahoma Press, 1954.

Cox, J. C., and C. B. Ford. *Parish Churches.* Rev. by Bryan Little. London, B. T. Batsford, Ltd., 1966.

Davidson, Marshall B. *The American Heritage History of Colonial Antiques.* New York, American Heritage Publishing Company, Inc., 1967.

Davis, J. *The First Settlers of Virginia.* New York, Riley and Company, 1806.

Devon, Frederick. *Pell Records James I.* London, John Rodwell, 1836.

Dickens, Charles. *A Child's History of England.* New York, G. W. Carleton & Co., 1878.

Drake, Francis S., ed. *The Indian Tribes of the United States.* Philadelphia, J. B. Lippincott and Company, 1884.

Drake, Samuel G. *The Aboriginal Races of North America*. 15th ed. New York, Hurst and Company, 1880.

Dutt, W. A. *The King's Homeland*. London, Adam and Charles Black, 1904.

Dutton, Ralph. *The English Country House*. Rev. ed. London, B. T. Batsford, Ltd., 1962.

Embrey, Alvin T. *History of Fredericksburg, Virginia*. Richmond, Va., Old Dominion Press, 1937.

Fiske, John. *Old Virginia and Her Neighbors*. 2 vols. Boston, Houghton Mifflin Company, 1897.

Force, Peter. *Tracts and Other Papers, Relating Principally to the Origin, Settlement, and Progress of the Colonies in North America from the Year of Discovery of the Country to the Year 1776*. 3 vols. Washington, Force, 1836.

Foreman, Carolyn Thomas. *Indians Abroad*. Norman, University of Oklahoma Press, 1943.

Garnett, David. *Pocahontas, or the Nonparell of Virginia*. London, Chatto and Windus, 1933.

Goodman, Godfrey. *The Court of King James The First*. 2 vols. London, 1839.

Green, John Richard. *History of the English People*. 2 vols. New York, American Book Exchange, 1881.

Groves, G. I. *Famous American Indians*. Chicago, 1944.

Gruden, Robert Pierce. *History of Gravesend*. London, William Pickering; James Johnston, Gravesend, 1843.

Guide Book King's Lynn England. King's Lynn, King's Lynn Publicity Committee, 1933.

Hamer, Philip M., ed. *A Guide to Archives and Manuscripts in the United States*. New Haven, Yale University Press, 1961.

History of the Thirteen Colonies. New York, American Heritage Publishing Company, Inc., 1967.

Horgan, Paul. *The Habit of Empire*. Santa Fe, N.M., Rydal Press, Inc., 1939.

Hotten, John Camden. *The Original Lists of Persons of Quality . . . and Others Who Went from Great Britain to the American Planta-*

tions, 1600–1700 (compiled from "MSS. Preserved in the State Paper Dept. of Her Majesty's Public Record Office, London"). New York, G. A. Baker Company, 1874.

Hyde, George E. *Indians of the Woodlands: From Prehistoric Times to 1725.* Norman, University of Oklahoma Press, 1962.

Irving, Washington. *The Life and Voyages of Christopher Columbus.* ("Arundel Series," No. 134.) New York, United States Book Company, 1891.

Jacobson, Jerome, S.J. *Educational Foundations of the Jesuits in Sixteenth Century New Spain.* Berkeley, University of California Press, 1938.

———. *James I, King of Great Britain.* 1690.

Jones, Mrs. Herbert. *Sandringham Past and Present.* London, Sampson Low, Marston, Searle, and Livingston, 1883.

King's Lynn, England. London, for John Franke, 1642.

Knight, Frank, and Rutley Knight. *Heacham Hall.* London, Waterlow & Sons, Ltd., 1929.

Larned, Josephus Nelson. *The New Larned History for Ready Reference.* 6 vols. Springfield, Mass., 1901.

———, ed. *The Literature of American History.* Boston, Houghton Mifflin Company, 1902.

Lewis, Clifford M., S.J., and Albert J. Loomis, S.J. *The Spanish Jesuit Mission in Virginia 1570–1572.* Chapel Hill, University of North Carolina Press, 1953.

Linklater, Eric. *Ben Jonson and King James.* London, 1931.

McElwee, William. *History of England.* New York, Barnes & Noble, Inc., 1960.

McKenney, Thomas L., and James Hall. *The Indian Tribes of North America.* Intro. by H. S. Braunholtz. Edinburgh, John Grant Publishers, 1934.

McSpadden, J. Walker. *Indian Heroes.* New York, 1928.

Mason, Frances Norton. *My Dearest Polly.* Richmond, Va., Garrett & Massie, Inc., 1961.

Meade, William. *Old Churches, Ministers and Families of Virginia.* 2 vols. Philadelphia, J. B. Lippincott Company, 1894.

Neill, Edward D. *History of the Virginia Company of London, with Letters to and from the First Colony Never Before Printed.* Albany, Joel Munsell, 1869. (From first relation of the colony, published in 1608 and attributed to John Smith.)

Nichols, John. *The Progresses, Processions and Magnificent Festivities of King James I . . . .* 4 vols. London, J. B. Nichols, 1828.

Nicholson, Nigel. *Great Houses of Britain.* New York, G. P. Putnam's Sons, 1965.

Nutting, Wallace. *Virginia Beautiful.* New York, Garden City, New York, Publishing Company, 1930.

Parley, Peter. *Lives of Celebrated American Indians.* Boston, Bradbury, Soden & Company, 1843.

Petrie, Sir Charles. *The Stuarts.* London, Eyre and Spottiswoode, 1937.

Price, Andrew. *The Princess Pocahontas.* Marlinton, W.Va., 1924.

Robertson, Wyndham. *Pocahontas and Her Descendants.* Richmond, Va., J. W. Randolph and English, 1887.

Scherman, David E., and Rosemarie Redlich. *Literary America.* New York, Dodd, Meade & Company, Inc., 1952.

Schoolcraft, Henry, *Algic Researches.* New York, Harper & Brothers, 1839.

Seelye, Elizabeth Eggleston, and Edward Eggleston. *Pocahontas.* New York, 1879.

Shelley, Henry C. *Inns and Taverns of Old London.* London, Sir Isaac Pitman and Sons, Ltd., 1809.

Smith, John. *Travels and Works of Captain John Smith.* Ed. by Edward Arber and A. G. Bradley. 2 vols. Edinburgh, John Grant Publishers, 1910.

Smith, Lacey Baldwin. *The Horizon Book of the Elizabethan World.* New York, American Heritage Publishing Company, Inc., 1967.

Stacy, John. *A General History of the County of Norfolk.* 2 vols. London, John Stacy, 1829.

Stith, William. *The History of the First Discovery and Settlement of Virginia.* Williamsburg, William Parks, 1746.

Swem, E. G. *Virginia Historical Index.* 2 vols. Roanoke, Stone Printing and Manufacturing Company, 1934.

Taylor, William. *The History and Antiquities of Castle Rising.* London, J. Masters; [King's] Lynn, W. Taylor and Thew and Son, 1850.

This England. Foreword by Melville Bell Grosvenor. Washington, National Geographic Society, 1966.

Thwaites, Reuben Gold, ed. *The Jesuit Relations and Allied Documents, 1612–1614.* Vol. II. Cleveland, Burrows Brothers Company, 1896.

Weddell, Alexander Wilbourne, ed. *A Memorial Volume of Virginia Historical Portraiture 1558–1830.* Richmond, Va., 1930.

Willson, George F. *Saints and Strangers.* New York, Reynal & Hitchcock, 1945.

Wilson, Arthur. *The History of Great Britain.* London, for Richard Lownds, 1653.

Wilson, John Dover. *Life in Shakespeare's England.* Baltimore, Penguin Books, Inc., 1959.

Winsor, Justin, ed. *Narrative and Critical History of America.* Vol. IV. Boston, 1884.

Woods, George B., Homer A. Watt, and George K. Anderson. *The Literature of England.* Rev. ed. Vol. I. Chicago, Scott, Foresman & Company, 1941.

Wright, Louis B. *Shakespeare for Everyman.* New York, Washington Square Press, Inc., 1964.

V. BOOKLETS

General History

Abbot, William W. *A Virginia Chronology, 1585–1783.* Richmond, Garrett & Massie, Inc., 1957.

Bland, Edward (Merchant), Abraham Woods, Captaine Sackford Brewster, and Elias Pennant, Gentlemen. *A Discovery of New Britaine.* Ann Arbor, reprinted for the Clements Library Associates, 1960. (Originally published in London in 1651).

Brydon, Rev. G. Maclaren (historiographer of the Episcopal Diocese of Virginia). *Highlights Along the Road of the Anglican Church.* Richmond, Va., Virginia Diocesan Library, 1957.

———. *Religious Life of Virginia in the Seventeenth Century.* Richmond, Va., Garrett & Massie, Inc., 1957.

The Church of Saint Mary, the Virgin, Heacham, Bishop's House, Norwich, England, Heacham Parochial Church Council, 1963.

Harrison, Caroline Rivers. *Historic Guide Richmond and James River.* 9th ed. Richmond, 1961.

Henrico County Primary and Secondary Highway Systems. Richmond, Va., Department of Highways, January 1, 1963.

Herndon, Melvin. *Tobacco in Colonial Virginia, "The Sovereign Remedy."* Richmond, Va., Garrett & Massie, Inc., 1957.

Hiscock, Robert Heath. *A History of the Parish Churches of Gravesend and the Burial Place of Princess Pocahontas.* Gloucester, England, n.d.

Hughes, Thomas P. *Medicine in Virginia 1607–1699.* Richmond, Va., Garrett & Massie, Inc., 1957.

Hunt, David C. *Reports from the New World.* Tulsa, Thomas Gilcrease Institute of American History and Art, 1966.

Johns, Ann Page. *The Rolfe Property, Warren House, at "Smith's Fort Plantation" 1652–1935.* Richmond, Va., Association for the Preservation of Virginia Antiquities, 1938.

McCary, Ben C. *Indians in Seventeenth-Century Virginia.* Richmond, Va., Garrett & Massie, Inc., 1957.

———. *John Smith's Map of Virginia, with a Brief Account of Its History.* Richmond, Va., Garrett & Massie, Inc., 1957.

Quarles, Marguerite Stuart. *Pocahontas: Bright Stream Between Two Hills.* Richmond, Va., Association for the Preservation of Virginia Antiquities, 1939.

Syon House. Northhampton, England, Syon House Estate, 1950.

Williams, Frances Leigh. *A Tour of Historic Richmond.* Richmond, Va., 1937.

Tudor and Stuart Civilization

LaMar, Virginia A. *English Dress in the Age of Shakespeare.* Washington, Folger Shakespeare Library, 1958.

———. *Travel and Roads in England.* Washington, Folger Shakespeare Library, 1960.

Penrose, Boies. *Tudor and Early Stuart Voyaging.* Washington, Folger
Shakespeare Library, 1962.

Schmidt, Albert J. *The Yeoman in Tudor and Stuart England.* Washington, Folger Shakespeare Library, 1961.

Stone, Lilly C. *English Sports and Recreations.* Washington, Folger
Shakespeare Library, 1960.

Thompson, Craig R. *The English Church in the Sixteenth Century.*
Ithaca, Cornell University Press, 1958.

VI. ARTICLES

Andrews, K. R. "Christopher Newport of Limehouse, Mariner," *William and Mary Quarterly,* 3d Ser., Vol. XI, No. 1, 28–41.

Anonymous. "Orapax," *Virginia Magazine of History and Biography,*
Vol. XXXV (1937), 78.

Bushnell, David I., Jr. "John White—the First English Artist to Visit
America, 1585," *Virginia Magazine of History and Biography,* Vol.
XXXV (1937), 419–30.

———. "Virginia—from Early Records," *American Anthropologist,*
Vol. 9, No. 1 (January–March, 1907), 38–41.

Carter, Charles S. "Gondamar: Ambassador to James I," *Historical
Journal,* Vol. VII, No. 2 (1964), 189–208.

Cleaveland, The Rev. George J. "The Beginning of a Good Work," *Virginia Churchman,* Vol. LXX, No. 6 (December, 1961), 12–14.

———. "The Reverend Alexander Whitaker, M.A. Parson of Henrico,
Apostle to the Indians, a Saviour of Virginia," *Virginia Churchman,*
Vol. LXVI, No. 2 (June, 1957), 15–24.

Fisher, Allen C., Jr. "The City—London's Storied Square Mile," *National Geographic,* Vol. 129, No. 6 (June, 1966), 743–91.

Fishwick, Marshall. "Was John Smith a Liar?" *American Heritage,*
Vol. IX, No. 6 (October, 1958), 28–33, 110–11.

Goodwin, Mary F. "Virginia Ever Missionary," *Virginia Churchman,*
Vol. LXVI, No. 2 (June, 1957), 19–24.

Grossman, Mary Louise. "A Heritage in Peril," *American Heritage,*
Vol. XVII, No. 5 (August, 1966), 4–14, 68–69.

Hanke, Lewis. "Conquest and the Cross," *American Heritage,* Vol.
XIV, No. 2, (February, 1963), 5–17.

Hume, Ivor Noel. "Digging Up Jamestown," *American Heritage*, Vol. XIV, No. 3 (April, 1963), 66–77.

Kenney, Nathaniel T., and Bates Littlehales. "Chesapeake Country," *National Geographic*, Vol. 126, No. 3 (September, 1964), 370–411.

Land, Robert Hunt. "Henrico and Its College," *William and Mary Quarterly*, 2d Ser., Vol. VIII, 464–68.

Mooney, James. "The Powhatan Confederacy, Past and Present," *American Anthropologist*, Vol. 9, No. 1 (January–March, 1907), 123–29.

Morton, Louis, "The End of Formalized Warfare," *American Heritage*, Vol. VI, No. 5 (August, 1955), 12–15, 18–19, 95.

Price, Willard, and Robert F. Sisson, "The Thames Mirrors England's Varied Life," *National Geographic*, Vol. CXIV, No. 1 (July, 1958), 45–95.

Robinson, Morgan P. "Henrico Parish in Diocese of Virginia and the Parishes Descended Therefrom," *Virginia Magazine of History and Biography*, Vol. XLIII, No. 1 (January, 1935).

Rolfe, John. "John Rolfe's Will, of James City in Virginia, Dated 10 March 1621 . . . ," *Virginia Magazine of History and Biography*, Vol. XXI (1913), 209.

Rowse, A. L. "The Elizabethans and America," *American Heritage*, Vol. X, No. 3 (April, 1959), 4–15, 94–98; Vol. X, No. 4 (June, 1959), 4–19, 105–11; Vol. X, No. 5 (August, 1959), 22–29, 105–11; Vol. X, No. 6 (October, 1959), 48–53, 78–83; Vol. XI, No. 1 (December, 1959), 46–48, 57–59.

Russell, Frances. "Apostle to the Indians," *American Heritage*, Vol. IX, No. 6 (December, 1957), 4–9, 117–19.

Smythe, Clem T. "The Burial of Pocahontas," *Virginia Historical Register*, Vol. II (1849), 187–89.

Villiers, Alan, and Bates Littlehales. "Channel Cruise to Glorious Devon," *National Geographic*, Vol. 124, No. 2 (August, 1963), 208–59.

Willoughby, Charles C. "The Virginia Indians in the Seventeenth Century," *American Anthropologist*, Vol. 9, No. 1 (January–March, 1907), 57, 53n.

Wright, Louis B. "The Ancestors and Descendants of John Rolfe with Notices of Some Connected Families," *Virginia Magazine of History and Biography*, Vol. XXI (1913), 209–12.

————. "The Britain That Shakespeare Knew," *National Geographic*, Vol. 125, No. 5 (May, 1964), 613–67.

VII. INTERVIEWS

The Rev. George J. Cleaveland (registrar of the Episcopal Diocese of Virginia), Richmond, June, 1964.

Robert A. Elder, Jr. (museum specialist, Department of Anthropology, U.S. National Museum), Washington, June, 1964.

A. E. Gunther (author of *The Rolfe Family Records*, Vols. I and III), Heacham, Norfolk, England, May 20, 1968.

John Waverly Lindsey (owner and occupant of site of Werowocomoco), June, 1964.

Ben C. McCary (professor of modern languages in the College of William and Mary), Williamsburg, June, 1964.

Howard A. MacCord, Sr. (archaeologist, Virginia State Library, Richmond), June, 1964.

Relatives of Tecumseh Cook, chief of the Pamunkey Indians, living on the Pamunkey Reservation: Mrs. Jayce Bradby, a niece; Mrs. Dora Bradby, a sister; and Pocahontas Cook, a sister, June, 1964.

T. Dale Stewart (acting curator, physical anthropology, Smithsonian Institution, and author of "The Finding of an Indian Ossuary on the York River in Virginia," *Journal of the Washington Academy of Science*, Vol. XXX [1940], 356–64; and of "Excavating the Indian Village of Patawomeke [Potomac]," *Explorations and Field Work of the Smithsonian Institution in 1938* [1938–40], 87–90), June, 1964.

VIII. ETHNOLOGICAL SPECIMENS FROM TIDEWATER VIRGINIA

Department of Antiquities, Ashmolean Museum, Oxford

Powhatan's mantle, heavily embroidered with roanoke figures of animals and men.

Pocahontas

Bow, arrows, quivers, darts (*ca.* 1607–1608).
Purse, typical of those worn by Powhatan males in Pocahontas' era, embroidered in roanoke perforated with an awl and sewed to purse with sinew thread.
Tobacco pipes.

Smithsonian Institution, Washington

Beads (bone and shell).
Imprinted pottery fragments.
Pipes.
Miscellaneous artifacts.

Jamestown, Virginia

Double white shell earrings edged with silver, supposedly reset for Pocahontas by the Earl of Northumberland when she visited him at the Tower of London in 1616.
Pocahontas' small sewing basket, ornamented with porcupine quills.
Indian trade artifacts relating to English-Indian trade in the seventeenth century: beads, bells, hatchets, scissors, knives.
English artifacts: metal farming tools; hardware for houses; brick and other building materials; military weapons (fragments), such as gun parts, polearms, cutlasses, and broadswords; suits of mail and armor; and earthenware, glass, and metal objects of English manufacture.

Pamunkey Indian Reservation, King William County, Virginia

From private collection of Tecumseh Cook, chief of the Pamunkey Indians:
Pottery.
Pipes.
Bows, arrows, clubs, and other early Pamunkey weapons.
Awls, scrapers, stone chisels, and other tools, both artifacts and reproductions.

Index

Abbot, Jeffry: 99
Abnaki Indians: 172n.
Accomac County, Va.: 37
Ahone (Powhatan deity): 14–15, 158
Algonquian Indians: 9ff.; ties with
  Powhatans, 9–10, 11; language of,
  10; architecture of, 10; clothing of,
  12–13; conquered by Chief
  Powhatan, 17
Alicock, Jeremy: 60–61
Amopotoiske (Chief Powhatan's wife):
  39

"Ancients," the: see Jamestown
  colonists
Anglicanism: 47, 57, 185
Anne, Queen (wife of James I): 62,
  170, 176ff., 192, 193
Apamatuks (Powhatan village): 70,
  135, 136
Apostle's Creed: 159
Appomattoc (Powhatan village): 16
Appomattoc Indians: 94
Archer, Gabriel: 75, 80n., 113
Architecture: Powhatan, 10, 66 & n.,

215

67, 71, 85 & n., 126, 158n.;
English, in Jamestown, 52; use of
pine in English, 58–59n.
Argall, Capt. Samuel: 112, 113, 130,
131, 140, 153ff., 164, 186 & n., 188;
plots to abduct Pocahontas, 153;
attends Pocahontas' funeral, 185
Armor, used by colonists: 57–58
Arrohattoc (Powhatan village): 16
Art and artifacts, Indian: 9 & n., 39
Asbie, John: 60
Ashetoiske (Chief Powhatan's wife):
39
Ashmolean Museum (Oxford
University): 90 n.

Bacon, Sir Francis: 113n.
Battle, John S.: 193
Bell Savage Inn (London, England):
175, 178
Bermuda: 121 ff., 131, 161 & n.
Bermuda Hundred, Va.: 138, 155, 165
Bible: 57
Blackwater River: 37
Blair family (Virginia): 191
Blue Ridge Mountains: 38n.
Bohun, Dr. Laurence: 126
Bolling family (Virginia): 191
Book of Common Prayer: 57, 185
Bottom Bridge, Va.: 64
Brentford, England: 180
Brentford Inn (Brentford, England):
180
Brewster, Capt. Edward: 136
"Bright Stream Between Two Hills":
see Pocahontas
Brinton, Edward: 87
Brumfield, James: 5
Bruster, William: 60
Bucke, Rev. Richard: 121, 125, 126,
135, 165
Buckingham, Earl of: 182
Buckler, Andrew: 87
Burras, Anne: 86

Callamata, Lady: 181
Cambridge University: 161 & n.

Canai Indians: 38n.
Canterbury, England: 171 n.
Cape Fear, N.C.: 42
Cape Hatteras, N.C.: 42
Cape Henry, Va.: 48
Carleton, Sir Dudley: 60 n., 157n.,
175, 177n., 182, 186
Cassen, George: 64, 65 & n.
Cassen, William: 52
Cecil, Robert: 113n., 114n., 126
Chamberlain, John: 60 n., 157n., 175,
177n., 182, 185
Charles V, King: 42
Charles, Prince (son of James I): 170,
176 & n.
Cherokee Indians: 9
Chesapeake Bay: 10, 38, 42ff., 48, 85,
131
Chesapeake Indians: 44
Chickahominy Indians: 45, 112, 169,
190; barter with colonists, 76; attack
Jamestown, 114
Chickahominy River: 6, 40 n., 49,
63ff.
Chickasaw Indians: 9
Children of the Queens Revels: 121
Chiskiack Indians: 96, 114
Choctaw Indians: 9
Christianity: 4, 178n., 192; *see also*
religion
Church of England: 134–35, 158ff.,
172; *see also* Anglicanism
Church of St. Mary the Virgin
(Heacham, England): 193
Cinquoteck, Va.: 68n.
"Cleopatre" (Thomas Rolfe's
Powhatan aunt): 191
Clothing: 89, 126, 169; worn by In-
dians, 12–13, 67n., 69n., 70, 136,
174n., 177; worn by Jamestown
colonists, 53; worn by Pocahontas,
82, 165, 177, 181, 193; worn by
Chief Powhatan, 77–78, 87; worn in
Powhatan drama, 88; sent by Chief
Powhatan to King James, 90 & n.;
worn by Thomas Rolfe, 181
Clovell, Eustis: 6

College Creek: 43
Collier, Samuel: 5, 87
Colonization by Europeans: 4, 41 ff.;
    see also Jamestown, Va.; New
    World; Virginia
Conestoga Indians: *see* Susquehanna
    Indians
Conoy Indians: 38n.
Constitution and Canons of the
    Province of Canterbury: 57
Copes, Sir William: 60n.
Corn: *see* food
Cornwallis, Lord: 193
Coronado, Francisco Vásquez de: 4
Cortés, Hernando: 4
Court of St. James's: 119
Crashaw, Rev. William: 124, 170
Creek Indians: 9
Cuba: 43, 44

Dale, Sir Thomas: 127, 135n., 161n.,
    162, 165, 169, 183n.; assumes tem-
    porary command of colony, 127,
    133ff.; plans new settlements, 135,
    138; burns Queen Oppussoquion-
    uske's village, 138; his role of, in Po-
    cahontas' abduction, 153ff., 164;
    instructs Pocahontas in Christianity,
    159; approves of Rolfe's marriage to
    Pocahontas, 163; offers to "marry"
    Chief Powhatan's daughter, 166;
    tries to help finance Jamestown, 168;
    suggests that Pocahontas visit Eng-
    land, 172; organizes Pocahontas'
    retinue, 174–75n.; brings Pocahon-
    tas to England, 175; visits the Rolfes
    in England, 179
Delaware: 132
Delaware River: 10
De La Warr (ship): 124, 126
De La Warr, Lady: 177
De La Warr, Lord Thomas West: 116,
    123ff., 131ff.; appointed governor
    of Jamestown, 113; plans rehabilita-
    tion of Jamestown, 125; instructed
    to convert Indians, 139–40; acts as
    Pocahontas' social sponsor, 177

Deliverance (ship): 120, 121, 123
De Soto, Hernando: 4
Discovery (ship): 4–5, 54, 60, 61,
    75ff., 80n.
Diseases of Jamestown colonists:
    60–61, 126
Donne, John: 170
Dutch Gap, Va.: 137

Elizabeth (ship): 161
Elizabeth City, Va.: 155
Elizabeth I, Queen: 53, 170
Emry, Thomas: 52, 64, 65, 75
England: 112, 113, 126, 127, 160,
    161n., 166, 170n., 171 & n., 179n.;
    and relationship of English to Poca-
    hontas, 3, 4, 6, 155, 157n., 162, 168,
    172 & n., 174–83, 191–93; New
    World settlements founded by, 3, 4,
    41ff., 85, 118ff., 134, 138, 170; and
    plot to capture Powhatans, 139–40,
    153; *see also* Jamestown, Va.; James-
    town colonists; Pocahontas; Virginia

Falcon (ship): 113
Farrar's Island, Va.: *see* Henrico, Va.
Fermoy, Lord: 193
Flowre, George: 60
Food: 9, 77ff., 93, 97, 100, 153, 156;
    of Powhatans, 15, 70; used as tax
    payment, 38, 39; of colonists, 59, 61,
    63, 67, 125, 131–32; brought from
    England, 74, 76; destroyed by fire,
    76; supplied by Pocahontas, 76;
    colonists' lack of, 93; eaten by rats,
    94; obtained from Indians, 95, 96,
    115; obtained from Opechancan-
    ough, 109–10; planting of, 112, 188;
    cannibalism at Jamestown, 117, 120;
    grain supply assured for colonists,
    138; *see also* Jamestown colonists,
    Powhatan Indians
Forest, Mrs. (Jamestown colonist):
    86
Fort Charatie, Va.: 158n.
Fort Charles, Va.: 133
Fort Elizabeth, Va.: 158n.

Fort Henry, Va.: 133
Fort James, Va.: 190–91n.
Fort Mount Malady, Va.: 158n.
Fort Patience, Va.: 158n.
France: 176; gives gifts to Susquehannocks, 85; opposes English settlements, 138
Francis I, King (France): 42
Frankwell, Rev. Nicholas: 185
.Fredericksburg, Va.: 37
Furnishings: 87, 116, 126

Gates, Sir Thomas: 121 ff., 133, 136, 155, 158n., 161n.; plays part in abduction of Pocahontas, 153ff.; tries to help finance Jamestown, 168
Generall Historie of Virginia, New-England, and the Summer Isles, The (book): 56, 71n., 181
George (ship): 184
Godspeed (ship): 4–5, 58, 60, 61n.
Gold, search for: 82 & n., 86n.
Goldstone, Dr. (of Henrico, Va.): 183n.
Gómez, Estéban: 42
Good Speed to Virginia (publication): 119
Gosnold, Anthony: 100
Gosnold (Gosnoll), Capt. Bartholomew: 61
Government of Jamestown, Va.: *see* Jamestown, Va.
Government of Powhatan Indians: *see* Powhatan Indians
Grand Assembly of Virginia: 190n.
Gravesend, England: 184 & n., 186, 187, 192ff.
Gray's Creek: 190
Gray's Inn (London): 75
Great Lakes: 4
Grenville, Sir Richard: 44
Gunpowder Plot: 54
Gunther, A. E.: 193

Hailsham, Lord: 193
Hakluyt, Richard: 48
Hamor, Raphe: 137, 154, 166, 185

Hampton, Va.: *see* Kecoughtan
Hariot, Thomas: 11
Haslam, Rev. John H.: 192
Heacham, Diocese of (England): 161n.
Heacham, England: 181, 193, 194
Heacham Hall (Rolfe ancestral home): 161n.
Henrico, Va.: 154, 155, 158 & n., 160, 165, 183n.; establishment of, 135–36; construction of, 137, 138; description of, 137; plans for school in, 183, 189
Henry, Prince (son of King James I): 136, 176n.
Horton, Mrs. (Jamestown colonist): 121, 161n.
House of Lords (English): 54
Housing: *see* architecture
Hudson River: 10
Hunt, Rev. Robert: 57, 76, 85n., 121

Indians: *see* names of families, individuals, and tribes
"Indian Sea": 48, 64, 85n.
Infanta María (Spain): 170
Instructions, Orders, and Constitutions (for Jamestown colony): 140
Ireland: 54, 123, 176
Iroquoian family: 9, 38n.
Isle of Hogs (in James River): 100
Isle of Wight County, Va.: 95

"Jack of the Feathers": *see* Chief Munetute
James I, King (England): 45n., 47, 54, 65, 176n., 178 & n., 179n., 182, 192; visited by Pocahontas, 4; outlines rules for settlement of Virginia, 48, 86–87; oath of allegiance to, 49 & n., 55; sends gifts to Chief Powhatan, 89, 126; receives gift of flying squirrels, 114n.; opposes John Rolfe's marriage, 169; attitude toward Jamestown colony, 169–71
James River: 6, 16, 38n., 42 & n., 43,

45n., 49, 59, 61, 77, 95, 100, 123, 133ff., 165, 190

Jamestown, Va.: 11 & n., 12, 37, 51–62, 64, 68ff., 74, 75, 81ff., 85 & n., 86, 90ff., 100, 110ff., 120, 129, 136, 140, 153ff., 161 & n., 167, 170, 171, 179, 190, 194; saved by Pocahontas, 4; visited by Pocahontas, 4–5, 176; activities of settlers in 4–5; fort at, 4, 6, 67 & n., 68n.; attacked by Paspaheghs, 6, 50, 54; settlement of, 48, 49, 51, 176; buildings in, 52; new settlers arrive at, 74, 75, 81, 86, 122; fire at, 76; rebuilding of, 77, 85; Edward Maria Wingfield reports on, 80n.; reasons for colonization of, 85; women arrive at, 86; selected for Chief Powhatan's coronation, 86ff.; John Smith's policies for, 110, 111, 112; second charter received for, 112-13; new governing body for, 113, 133; revitalization of, 113, 125–26, 128, 131, 133; involvement in Powhatan's War, 114ff., 129; apparent death of, 118ff.; salvation of, 120; plans made for abandonment of, 123; visited by Lord De La Warr, 123; return of colonists to, 124; new policies established for, 127, 133–34; order returns to, 135; new settlements near, 135; Pocahontas taken to, 155ff.; scene of Pocahontas' wedding, 165; monetary problems of, 170–72; attacked by Powhatans, 189–90; relations of, with Powhatans, 191; site of Pocahontas statue, 194; *see also* Jamestown colonists, Pocahontas, John Smith, Virginia

Jamestown colonists: 3ff., 11, 14, 16, 38ff., 41, 47, 70, 111, 114; relationship with Pocahontas, 3–4, 39, 51–53, 55, 61, 62, 63, 72, 73, 76, 77, 81, 82, 87–89, 91, 99–100, 109, 110, 131, 139, 155, 192; attacked by Paspaheghs, 6, 54; relationship with Powhatans, 4, 6, 40, 41, 46ff., 55ff., 76, 78ff., 84, 87ff., 92ff., 111, 126,
135, 138, 139, 164; attempt to find Roanoke survivors, 45n.; arrive in Powhatan country, 46; settle Jamestown, 48, 49, 51, 176; physical description of, 53; occupations of, 53, 136; bring gifts for Indians, 56; try to convert Powhatans, 57, 130–40; religion of, 57, 125–26, 140; armor of 57–58; lack of supplies, 58 & n., 59, 93, 94, 117, 126; strife among, 59, 60 & n.; deaths among, 60–61, 74–75, 117, 126; barter with Powhatans, 76–77; search for gold, 82 & n., 86n.; rebuild Jamestown, 85, 112, 126; arrival of, 74ff., 86, 122; entertained by Powhatans, 87–88; illness of, 93, 115, 126; plagued by rats, 94–95; visit Wcrowocomoco, 95 & n., 96; plotted against by Chief Powhatan, 99; sent out by John Smith to prove self-sufficiency, 112; attacked in Powhatan's War, 114, 115, 136ff.; ambushed by Chief Powhatan, 116–17, 128; prepare to abandon Jamestown, 123; return to Jamestown, 124; punishment of, 133–34; goals for, 134; help build new settlement, 136, 137; become friends of Patawomeke Indians, 138; abduct Pocahontas, 153ff.; visit Pocahontas in London, 179; grieve at Pocahontas' death, 186; reconfirm peace with Powhatans, 188; attacked by Powhatans, 189–90; *see also* architecture; clothing; food; Jamestown, Va.; Pocahontas; Chief Powhatan; Powhatan Indians; Powhatan's War; religion; names of specific persons

Jamestown Peninsula: 58, 112, 120, 124, 128, 132–33; *see also* Jamestown, Va.

Japazeus: *see* Jopassus

Jesuit missionaries: 43; *see also* Father Juan Segura

Jewelry: 12, 13, 79, 80 & n., 98, 179, 181, 194

Jonson, Ben: 172–73, 179, 182
Jopassus (Patawomeke Indian): 154, 155

Kecatough (Pocahontas' uncle): 68n.
Kecoughtan (Powhatan village): 37, 44, 49, 77, 95
Kemps (Powhatan prisoner): 112
Kempster, Councillor L.: 193
Kendall, George: 60
King, John: 165, 170, 178
King's Council: 54
King's Lynn, England: 161n.
King William County, Va.: 16, 68 & n.

"Lady Rebecca": *see* Pocahontas
Lambeth Palace (London, England): 178
Lane, Ralph: 44
"Laws Devine, Morall, and Martiall" (of Jamestown): 133
Laxon, William: *see* William Laxton
Laxton (Laxon), William: 52, 112
Laydon, John: 52
Lenape Indians: 10, 38n.
Levitical law: 75
Lewis family (of Virginia): 191
"Little Snow Feather": *see* Pocahontas
"Little Wanton": *see* Pocahontas
Lizard (ship): 185
London, Bishop of: 165, 170, 172, 178
London, England: 113, 118, 121, 130, 158, 177n.; visited by Pocahontas, 174–80, 182–83; becomes home of Thomas Rolfe, 188
London, Lord Bishop of: *see* Bishop of London
London, Lord Mayor of: 118
London Company: 4, 138, 153
Lord's Prayer: 159
Lost Colony: *see* Roanoke colony
Low Countries: 54, 123, 133, 137
Ludgate Hill (London, England): 175
Lynn, Archdeacon of: 193

Mahican Indians: 10
Maine: 172n.

Manahoac Indians: 38n., 78
Manhattan Indians: 10
Martin, John: 60, 75, 80n., 82n.
Mary and Margaret (ship): 86
Maryland: 132
Matachanna (Pocahontas' half-sister): 174n., 186n.
Matchumps (Powhatan youth): 121, 122
Mattaponi (Indian village): 16
Mattaponi River: 16, 68n.
Matthew, Most Rev. Tobias: 119n.
Menapacant, Va.: *see* Menapucunt, Va.
Menapucunt, Va.: 68 & n., 69, 109
Menéndez de Avilés, Captain-General Pedro: 42–43
Mexico: 4, 43
Middlesex County, Va.: 68
Monacan Indians: 9, 38n., 78, 86n., 87, 93
Montezuma II: 4
Montgomery, Earl of: 182
Mulberry Island, Va.: 123
Munetute, Chief (Powhatan Indian): 136
Munsee Indians: 10
Muskhogean family: 9
Mutton, Richard: 5

Namontack (Powhatan youth): 79, 87ff., 121, 122
Nancy, Lady Astor: 193
Nansemond Indians: 94
Nansemond River: 94
Nantaquoud: *see* John Smith
Nanticoke Indians: 38n.
Nelson, Capt. Francis: 81
Netherlands: 123
Neuse River: 37
New England: 177n.
New England Trials (book): 175–76
New Kent County, Va.: 40n.
Newport, Capt. Christopher: 45n., 55, 58 & n., 59, 61n., 74ff., 79, 80 & n., 81, 85n., 86n., 87, 93, 115, 121, 123, 135 & n., 161n.; saves John Smith,

75; visits Chief Powhatan, 77, 79; visits other Indians, 80n.; returns to Jamestown, 86; explores Monacan country, 87; attends Chief Powhatan's coronation, 89, 90; returns to England, 92

"Newport, Father". *see* Capt. Christopher Newport

Newport, Thomas: *see* Thomas Savage

Newport News, Va.: 43

New World, colonization of: 41, 161; influenced by Pocahontas, 3–4, 157n., 159, 183, 191; by Spaniards, 4, 42ff., 170; by French, 4, 42; by English, 41ff., 56, 72, 85, 118ff., 131, 132, 138, 157n., 165, 167, 170n., 171, 179n., 183; exploration of, 42, 58n.; *see also* Jamestown, Va.; Jamestown colonists; Virginia

New York State: 10

"Nonesuch" (John Smith's planned home): 113

Norfolk County, England: 160

Northampton County, Va.: 37

North Carolina: 37, 132

Northumberland, Earl of: 54, 179ff., 194

North Virginia, settlement of: 48

North Virginia Company: 112–13

Nova Britannia (publication): 119

Okeus (Powhatan deity): 14, 47, 170–71n.

"Old Edward" (Jamestown colonist): 52

Old Point Comfort, Va.: *see* Point Comfort, Va.

Old World: 159

Olmos, Alonzo de: 43–44

Opechancanough (Pocahontas' uncle): 65 & n., 66, 67, 68n., 80n., 109, 110, 188, 191 & n.; threatened by John Smith, 109; leads uprising against colonists, 189–90

Opitchapan (Pocahontas' uncle): 68n., 165, 188

Oppussoquionuske, Queen (Pocahontas' aunt): 70, 135, 137

Orapaks (Powhatan village): 39–40n., 66ff.

Ottopomtacks (wife of Chief Powhatan): 39

Outer Banks (North Carolina): 11

Oxford University: 90n.

Paint, used by Indians: 12–13, 69n., 88, 114, 136, 174n.

"Painted Tally" (Lenape Indians): 10

Pamunkey (Powhatan village): 16

Pamunkey, King of: *see* Opechancanough

Pamunkey Indians: 45, 68 & n.

Pamunkey River: 16, 37, 40n., 41, 43, 45, 66, 68n., 77, 96, 116

Parahunt (Pocahontas' half-brother): 11n., 113ff.

Parish Council of Heacham (England): 194

Parliament (England): 53, 113n., 170

Paspahegh (Powhatan village): 50

Paspahegh Indians: 49; attack Jamestown, 6, 50, 55; barter with colonists, 76

Pasptanze (Powhatan chief): 129, 130, 154

Passe, Simon de: 177n.

Pastancy, King of: *see* Pasptanze

Patamack (Powhatan chief): 131

Patawomeke (Powhatan village): 130, 155

Patawomeke Indians: 129ff., 138, 153, 154, 188

Patience (ship): 120ff.

Peacock, Nathaniel: 5

"Penobscot, Mrs." (Abnaki Indian): 172n.

Percy, George: 112, 115, 116, 122ff.; describes Powhatans, 11; sees possible Roanoke descendant, 45n.; records Jamestown events, 45n., 50, 52, 59, 61, 114; description of, 54; flees England, 54; seeks corn for colonists, 94; attacks Opechancanough, 109; becomes president of colony, 113, 115, 127, 133; visits Pocahontas, 179

Persons, Elizabeth: 121

Petersburg, Va.: 16, 37

Phettiplace, William: 99

Philip II, King (Spain): 43

Philip III, King (Spain): 60, 119ff.

Phoenix (ship): 81, 82n.

Piankatank (Powhatan village): 37

Piankatank Indians: 37, 68

Piankatank River: 68

Pine, use of, by English: 58–59n.

Pipisco, wife of (Powhatan Indian): 13

Pising, Edward: 52

Plymouth, England: 174

Pocahontas: 3ff., 39–40, 45, 65, 68n., 70, 77, 82–83, 84, 97, 131, 174–75n., 186, 194–95; as Powhatan Indian princess, 3, 40; friendship of, with English colonists, 3ff., 51–53, 55, 61, 62, 63, 72, 73, 74ff., 81ff., 87–89, 91, 92, 99–100, 109, 110, 114, 128–29, 130, 132, 139, 186, 192; influence of, on colonization, 3–4, 157n., 159, 183, 191; daughter of Chief Powhatan, 4, 39, 40; saves Jamestown, 4; is converted to Christianity, 4, 159; marries John Rolfe, 4, 165; youth of, 4–5; playmates of, 4–5; influenced by Powhatan culture, 8ff., 40; half-sister of Parahunt, 11n.; birth of, 39; mother of, 39–40; names of, 40; friendship of, with John Smith, 55, 56, 61, 72, 76, 81–82, 84, 87–88, 96 & n., 110, 114; rescues John Smith, 63, 71 & n.; mediates between Smith and Chief Powhatan, 81–82; clothing worn by, 82, 165, 177, 181, 193; entertains Jamestown settlers, 87–88; tries to persuade father to visit Jamestown, 89; is forbidden to communicate with settlers, 91, 92, 128, 176; settles among Patawomekes, 129; abduction of, 153ff.; description of, 155–56, 156n., 177, 181; learns English customs, 158–59; friendship of, with John Rolfe, 162ff.; is returned to father, 163; sails to Werowocomoco, 164; gives birth to son, 168; receives annual stipend, 169, 189; visits England, 172–73, 172n., 174–80, 182–83; portrait of, 177, 177–78n., 181; illness of, 179–80, 182, 184–85; visits Brentford, 180; reunion of, with John Smith, 180–81; meets Rolfe's family, 181–82; plans return to Virginia, 184; death of, 185; funeral of, 185; writings about, 187; memorials to, 191–94; *see also* Chief Powhatan, Powhatan Indians

Pochins (Chief Powhatan's son): 37, 49, 61, 95

Poetan Bay: 164

Point Comfort, Va.: 96, 112, 132, 164

Ponnoiske (Chief Powhatan's wife): 39

Popham, Sir John: 48

Popular party (England): 171 & n., 172

Port Cotáge, Va.: 45n.

Potomac Creek: 129, 154, 155

Potomac Indians: *see* Patawomeke Indians

Potomac River: 38n., 41, 85n., 129, 131, 154

Potts, Richard: 114

Powell, Thomas: 121

Powhatan (Powhatan village): 11n., 37

Powhatan, Chief: 5, 16, 37ff., 38n., 47, 67, 68n., 69ff., 75–76, 77–78, 79 & n., 80n., 81, 84, 86, 87, 92, 93, 95, 96, 100, 109, 110, 111, 115, 116, 128, 129, 130, 131, 133, 135, 139, 153, 154, 155, 157n., 159, 163, 168, 175 & n., 178n., 180 & n., 192; father of Pocahontas, 4; description of, 16; as ruler, 16, 37ff.; probable birthplace of, 37; changes name from Wahunsonacock, 37; conquers Algonquian tribes, 37; creates Powhatan Confederacy, 37; conquers Piankatanks, 37; taxes tribes, 38, 39; royal temples of, 38; wives of, 39, 40; conquers Chesapeakes, 44; and destruction of Roanoke colony, 44, 45n.; spares John Smith, 71; adopts Smith, 71, 72; wants weapons and materials of settlers, 76–77, 78; wants to meet "Father Newport," 77; clothing worn by, 77–78, 87; receives gift from John Smith, 78; agrees to provide corn for colonists, 78; meets Captain Newport, 79; trades with settlers, 79, 80; steals from settlers, 80–81; coronation of, 86ff.; forbids Pocahontas to communicate with settlers, 91, 92, 128; becomes increasingly militant, 93–94, 111; barters with Smith, 94ff.; plans to massacre settlers, 99; tricks colonists, 111–12, 115–17; wages Powhatan's War, 115ff., 136; welcomes Henry Spelman, 116; forbids trade with colonists, 122; negotiates with settlers, 156–57, 163, 164; approves of Pocahontas' marriage, 164–65; rejects marriage of daughter to Thomas Dale, 166; ends Powhatan's War, 166–67; learns of Pocahontas' death, 188; death of, 188 & n.; leaves land to Thomas Rolfe, 190; *see also* Pocahontas, Powhatan Confederacy, Powhatan Indians, Powhatan's War

Powhatan Confederacy: 47, 48, 63, 68n., 129, 169; created by Chief Powhatan, 37; size and location of, 37; population of, 37–38; military protection for, 38 & n.; neighboring tribes of, 38n.; Chief Powhatan becomes "king" of, 86ff.; change in leadership of, 188; *see also* Chief Powhatan, Powhatan Indians

Powhatan Indians: 6, 8–16, 17–40, 38n., 41ff., 59, 63, 72, 75, 86, 92, 95, 100, 129, 135, 156, 164, 177, 190; relations of, with colonists, 4, 6, 40ff., 43ff., 49, 51, 55ff., 61, 63, 64,

76ff., 84, 85–86, 86n., 87–88, 89, 93ff., 109, 110, 111, 112, 114, 122–23, 135, 138, 139, 164, 191; religious practices of, 6, 8ff., 13ff., 68n., 69 & n., 93, 115, 171n., 183n.; culture of, 8–16, 37–40, 87–89, 114; origins of, 9; lack of records by, 9 & n.; as part of late Woodland culture, 9–10; utensils of, 9; neighbors of, 9; language of, 9–10, 55–56; ties of, with Algonquians, 9–10, 11; homes of, 10; hair styles of, 11, 13; description of, 11–12, 13; clothing worn by, 12–13, 67n., 69n., 70, 88, 174n.; food of, 15, 70; government of, 16, 37ff.; taxed by Powhatan, 38, 39; commodities of, 38–39; names of, 40; territory of, explored by Europeans, 41–43; killed by European settlers, 46; battle with colonists, 58, 114, 115, 117, 128, 136, 137, 138, 189–90; capture John Smith, 64–73; barter with settlers, 75ff., 80, 93; steal from colonists, 80–81; threaten colonists, 81; entertain Jamestown settlers, 87–88; ambush colonists, 117; to be converted by settlers, 139–40; reconfirm peace with settlers, 188; lose control of Tidewater Virginia, 191n.; *see also* food, Jamestown colonists, Pocahontas, Chief Powhatan, Powhatan Confederacy, Powhatan's War, Religion

Powhatan's Flu: *see* James River
Powhatan's River: *see* James River
Powhatan's War: 114ff., 127ff., 138, 153, 156, 166–67, 176
Poynt Comfort, Va.: *see* Point Comfort, Va.
Poythress, Jane: 191
Privy Council: 169
Providence Forge, Va.: 64
Purchas, Rev. Samuel: 171–72, 178, 183n., 188n.

Queens Creek: 43
Quiyoughcohanock Indians: 49, 61, 76

Raleigh, Sir Walter: 45n., 118, 178 & n., 179
Randolph, John: 191
Randolph family (Virginia): 191
Rappahannock (Powhatan village): 68
Rappahannock Indians: 45, 46, 68–69
Rappahannock River: 38n., 41, 45, 68, 85n.
Rasawrack (Chief Powhatan's home): 39–40n., 67, 115, 116, 129
Ratcliffe, Capt. John: 54, 80n., 113, 116–17; becomes council president, 60; condemns John Smith to death, 75
Rawhunt (Powhatan Indian): 72, 78
Read, James: 60
Rebecca: *see* Pocahontas
Redmayne, Robert: 161n.
Reincarnation: *see* religion of Powhatan Indians
Religion of English: 57, 115, 124ff., 134, 140, 158, 159, 170–71 & n., 185; *see also* Anglicanism, Christianity, Church of England, Roman Catholicism
Religion of Powhatan Indians: 6, 8ff., 13ff., 68n., 69 & n., 93, 115, 158, 171n., 183n.; theory of their creation, 13–14; belief in reincarnation, 14; belief in Okeus, 14; sacrifice of children, 14; belief in Ahone, 14–15; rituals in, 15–16; torture of captives, 15–16
Rich, Sir Robert: 179n.
Richmond, Va.: 16, 37, 86n.; *see also* Powhatan (Powhatan village)
Richmond County, Va.: 68
Roanoke Algonquians: 11; water-color drawings of, 11, 12; similarities to Powhatans, 11; hair styles of, 11, 13; description of, 11–12, 13
Roanoke colony: 4, 11, 44, 45n., 46, 47, 191; founded by English, 4; Indians of, 10–12; source of iron for Powhatans, 11n.; extermination of, 44; search for survivors of, 45n., 86n.; instructions for recovery of, 48

Roanoke Island: *see* Roanoke colony
Robinson, John: 64, 65, 75
Rochester, Bishop of (England): 192, 193
"Rocke Hall" (Rev. Alexander Whitaker's home): 158n.
Rodin, François Auguste René: 193
Rolfe, Bermuda (child of John Rolfe): 161n.
Rolfe, Edward: 161n.
Rolfe, Eustace: 161
Rolfe, Henry: 161n., 188
Rolfe, John: 158n., 160, 184, 186n., 192 & n., 194; marries Pocahontas, 4, 165; background of, 160–61; description of, 160–61; education of, 161 & n.; wants to establish tobacco industry in Virginia, 161; child of, 161n.; wife of, 161n.; friendship with Pocahontas, 162ff.; seeks Dale's permission to marry, 163; sails to Werowocomoco, 164; becomes recorder of colony, 169; arrives in Plymouth, England, 174; visits London, 174–80, 182–83; tries to help Sir Thomas Dale, 179n.; visits Brentford, 180; returns to Heacham, 181–82; attends Pocahontas' funeral, 185; returns to Virginia, 188; learns of Chief Powhatan's death, 188n.; seeks continuation of Pocahontas' stipend, 189; helps develop tobacco industry, 189; member of legislative assembly, 189; death of, 190; takes out patent on land for son, 190
Rolfe, Mrs. John: 161n.
Rolfe, Neville: 193
Rolfe, Rebecca: *see* Pocahontas
Rolfe, Thomas (son of Pocahontas and John Rolfe): 168–69, 174n.; arrives in Plymouth, 174; visits London, 174–80, 182–83; visits Brentford, 180; meets father's family, 181–82; description of, 181; plans return to Virginia, 184; illness of, 186n.; remains in England, 188; returns to Virginia, 190; inherited lands of,

190, 190–91 n.; becomes tobacco planter, 191; descendants of, 191, 193

Roman Catholicism: 43, 47, 49 & n., 54, 170–71; *see also* religion

Russell, Dr. Walter: 85n.

Russell, John: 98, 109

St. Augustine, Fla.: 43

St. George's Parish Church (Gravesend, England): 185, 192ff.

St. Lawrence River: 4

St. Martin's Church (England): 171

St. Paul's Cathedral (London): 171, 182

Samuel (English prisoner of Powhatans): 117, 129, 130

Sandys, Sir Edwin: 171 & n., 179, 182, 188, 189

Savage, Thomas: 79 & n., 89, 115, 116, 129, 130

Savannah River: 10

Scandinavia: 160

Scotland: 121

Scrivener, Matthew: 93ff., 100

Sea Venture (ship): 120–21, 121n., 123, 161n.

Sedgeford Hall Portrait of Pocahontas: 181

Segura, Father Juan: 43

Shakespeare, William: 121, 171

Shortridge, Jeffry: 117

Sicklemore, Capt. John: *see* Capt. John Ratcliffe

Siouan family: 9, 38n., 78

Small, Robert: 52

Smith, John: 16, 54ff., 60, 65n., 74, 76, 77, 80, 82n., 84–85, 86 & n., 89, 92–93, 95n., 100, 109, 111, 114, 115–16, 128–29, 177n., 180n.; relationship with Pocahontas, 5, 55, 56, 61, 62, 63, 72, 76, 81–82, 84, 87–89, 96 & n., 99–100, 110, 114, 186; description of, 55; background of, 55; arrest of, 55; knowledge of Powhatan language, 55–56, 65; rescued by Pocahontas, 63, 71 & n., 194; explores Chickahominy River, 64; captured by Powhatans, 64–73; spared by Chief Powhatan, 71; given country of Capahowosick, 71; adopted by Chief Powhatan, 71, 72; death sentence of, 75; visits Chief Powhatan at Werowocomoco, 77, 78, 79, 80; plans map of Powhatan country, 77n.; presents clothing to Chief Powhatan, 78; promises military aid to Chief Powhatan, 78; trades with other Indians, 80n.; helps remove Edward Maria Wingfield from office, 80n.; ends thievery by Powhatans, 81; captures Powhatans, 81; releases Powhatan prisoners, 82; elected president of Jamestown council, 84; attempts to increase colonization, 85; wounded by sting ray, 85n.; disapproves of plan to crown Chief Powhatan, 86–87, 90–91; supervises activities of new colonists, 86n.; plans for Chief Powhatan's coronation, 87, 89; entertained by Powhatans, 87–89; complains of lack of supplies, 93; tries to trade with Nansemonds, 94; barters with Chief Powhatan, 94ff.; goes to Werowocomoco to get corn, 95ff.; stays with Pochins, 95; stays with Chiskiacks, 96; plotted against by Chief Powhatan, 99; threatens Opechancanough, 109–10; establishes policies for Jamestown, 110, 111, 112; tries to prove self-sufficiency of colonists, 112; relinquishes presidency, 113; charged with mismanaging colony, 113; plans construction of new house, 113; burned by gunpowder explosion, 113; returns to England, 113, 114 & n.; writes about Pocahontas, 175–77, 187; reunited with Pocahontas, 180–81

Smithfield, Va.: 95

Smith's Fort, Va.: 190

Smythe, Sir Thomas: 5, 48, 135n., 182

Society of Colonial Dames of Virginia: 192

Somers, Sir George: 48, 121 ff.

Somerset, Earl of: 119n.

South America: 4

Southampton, Earl of: 171

South Virginia: 48–49; *see also* Tidewater Virginia

Spain: 4, 42 ff., 47, 60 & n., 119, 120, 138, 165, 169–70

Spanish Armada: 47, 161

Sparks, John: 164

Spelman, Henry: 115–16, 129 ff.

Stewart, T. Dale: 130 n.

Stingray Point, Va.: 85 n.

Stone Street (Gravesend, England): 184 n.

Strachey, William: 121, 125, 135; appointed recorder of Jamestown, 5; comments on Pocahontas, 5; description of Powhatans, 12, 13; comments on Chief Powhatan, 16; visits Chief Powhatan, 39

Strait of Belle Isle (Newfoundland): 10

Studley, Thomas: 59

Stukley, Sir Lewis: 174, 188

Suffolk County, Va.: 94

Supreme Council of the Virginia Company: 113, 125, 131, 134, 135 & n.

Surrey County, Va.: 190

Susan Constant (ship): 4–5, 45n., 55, 58, 60, 74, 76, 80

Susquehanna Indians: 38n., 85

Susquehanna River: 85

Swift, Ensign: 154, 155

Swift Creek: 16

"Symon" (English prisoner): 115

Symonds, Rev. William: 140, 170

Syon House (Brentwood, England): 180

Tackonekintaco (Powhatan chief): 95

Tankard, William: 114

Tapahanock Indians: *see* Quiyoughcohanock Indians

Tassore (Powhatan prisoner): 112

Tattooing, by Indian women: 13

Taxes, placed on Powhatans: 38, 39

Ten Commandments: 159

Thames River: 184 & n.

Tidewater Powhatans: *see* Powhatan Indians, Tidewater Virginia

Tidewater Virginia: 9 ff., 9n., 12 ff., 37, 38n., 132, 191n.; *see also* Algonquian Indians, Powhatan Indians, Roanoke Algonquians

Tobacco: 161–62, 165; used in Powhatan ceremonies, 15; introduction of, 138; developed by John Rolfe, 189

Todkill, Anas: 80 ff., 82n., 99

Tomocomo (Matachanna's husband): 174n.–175n., 182, 183n.

Tools and weapons: 9, 11 & n., 52, 58, 64, 65n., 68n., 71, 72, 76 ff., 85–86, 86n., 88 ff., 94 ff., 111, 112 & n., 113, 114, 126, 136–37, 156–57, 163, 164

Torrey, Mrs. Charles: 193, 194

Tower of London: 54, 178n., 179

Tragabigzanda, Lady: 181

Treasurer (ship): 154, 155, 164, 174

Treasurer and Company of Adventurers and Planters of the City of London for the First Colony in Virginia: 113 & n.

"True Relation of the State of Virginia, A" (Rolfe's tract): 182–83

U.S. House of Representatives: 191

U.S. Senate: 191

Uttamussack (Powhatan village): 38, 69, 116

"Varina" (Pocahontas' and John Rolfe's home): 165, 173, 190

Velasco, Alonso de: 120

Velasco, Don Luis de: 43

Verrazano, Giovanni da: 42

Virginia, English settlements in: 3–4, 11, 39–40, 41 ff., 50, 58, 60n., 61, 71n., 82, 114, 118, 119 & n., 120 ff., 131 ff., 153, 157n., 160, 168 ff., 175,

176, 182ff., 185, 188ff.; *see also* England; Jamestown, Va.; New World; North Virginia; Powhatan Indians; South Virginia; Tidewater, Va.; and specific locations

Virginia Company of London: 5, 161n., 163, 171; sponsors settlements in Virginia, 48, 56, 86, 87, 118ff., 132, 133, 170, 187, 188; receives second charter, 112–13; contemplates abduction of Powhatans, 139–40; provides stipend for Pocahontas, 169, 189; brings Pocahontas to England, 172ff.; learns of Pocahontas' death, 186; *see also* England; Jamestown, Va.; Virginia

Virginia General Assembly: 191

Virginia Richly Valued (publication): 119

Wahunsonacock: *see* Chief Powhatan
Waiman, Capt.: 60 & n.
Walam Olum: *see* "Painted Tally" (Lenape Indians)
Waldo, Capt. Richard: 87, 94, 100
Wallace, Ottillea: 193
Warman, Capt.: *see* Capt. Waiman
Warrasqueoc Indians: 95
Washington, D.C.: 37, 85n., 194
Waters, Robert: 121
Weanoc Indians: 65n., 76, 114
Weapons: *see* tools and weapons
Werowocomoco (Indian village): 15,

39, 69, 72, 75, 77 & n., 87ff., 93ff., 109, 116, 117, 164, 166
West, William: 112, 116–17
West Indies: 126, 178n.
West Point, Va.: 68n.
Weymouth, Capt. George: 172n.
Whitaker, Rev. Alexander: 134–35, 158 & n., 159, 162, 165, 170–71n., 188n.
White, John: 11, 12, 44
Whitechapel, England: 140
Whitehall (London, England): 182
White Oak Swamp (Virginia): 64
Wiffin, Richard: 99, 100, 109
Williamsburg, Va.: 43
William the Conqueror: 160
Windsor Shades, Va.: 64
Winganucki (wife of Chief Powhatan): 39
Wingfield, Edward Maria: 48, 49, 54, 59; unpopularity of, 54–55; removed from office, 60; imprisonment of, 60; returns to England, 80n.
Winne, Capt. Peter: 100, 111–12
"Wizard Earl": *see* Earl of Northumberland
Woodland culture: 9

York River: *see* Pamunkey River
Youghtanund (Powhatan village): 16, 37
Youghtanund Indians: 68

Zúñiga, Pedro de: 119, 121n.

The text for *Pocahontas* has been set on the Linotype in eleven-point Caledonia, one member of a distinguished family of types designed by W. A. Dwiggins, eminent American graphic artist.

The paper on which the book is printed bears the watermark of the University of Oklahoma Press and has an intended effective life of at least three hundred years.